THE YEAR 1000

THE YEAR

1000

Henri Focillon

HARPER TORCHBOOKS
Harper & Row, Publishers
New York, Evanston, San Francisco, London

This translation originally published in 1969 by Frederick Ungar Publishing Co., Inc. and is here reprinted by arrangement.

THE YEAR 1000

First HARPER TORCHBOOK edition published 1971

STANDARD BOOK NUMBER: 06-131609-1

Publisher's Note to the French Edition

THE *Year* 1000, the last work to be written by Henri Focillon, was interrupted by his death; he was not able to complete the archaeological chapters for which this material was to have served as an introduction. The publishers, however, do not feel that they are betraying the author's intentions by issuing this material separately as it stands, without its intended conclusion. It evokes with completeness the men and the problems of a pivotal epoch in the Western Middle Ages, an epoch for which Henri Focillon reserved a major place in his work and to which he devoted his last years as a teacher in France and in the United States.

Contents

List of Illustrations

THE YEAR 1000

Introduction

WE have often thought how useful it would be to historical inquiry, and generally to an understanding of mankind, if we were to take up a position at some fixed moment in time—not merely in order to examine that moment itself, but so that we might grasp in all their fullness the vistas that spread out around it: in other words, to make a survey of a site, a terrain which could then serve us as our point of observation. It has seemed both desirable and possible to us to choose a year, a climactic year, and first to empty it of its own content. The matter is more difficult than might appear at first glance—more suitably entrusted to the labors of a team than to the researches of a single historian. For, even a brief period of historic time comprises many layers or, if you will, stratifications. History is not the Hegelian future. History is not like a river on whose waters the events, and fragments of events, are carried along at the same pace and in the same direction. In fact, what we call history consists precisely in the diversity and unevenness of its currents. It should remind us rather of geological strata, laid one on top of the other, at various angles, broken here and there by sudden faults; here we can grasp in one place and at one time several of the earth's ages; and every moment of the time that has gone by is here at once past, present, and to come.

Obviously, such a stratigraphic analysis is bound to make us ask what came before and what after, or rather, to make us examine the moment we have chosen and seek in it the permanent presence of a more or less distinct past and the clear promise of a future. As we proceed, probing and drilling, we are inevitably led to see our point of observation not as a rigid edifice but, in its very structure, as a confluence of unequal movements. The vantage point from whose height we are trying to define a horizon is itself a rich and varied prospect.

What is a year? Measured by the motion of the stars, it is an absolute. But historically, things are not the same. Events do not occur within a year with the same regularity and frequency as the saints of the calendar. The year as it is lived by man and groups of men shares in man's lack of uniformity. Today its breath comes haltingly; tomorrow, in quick gasps. Its surface is at one time rippled, and at another time it billows. The year seems empty in one place, overfull in another. It overflows its banks and goes beyond its borders, or else it shrinks miserably into one or two spots surrounded by deserts which are often vast. It was a great idea of the Christian Church, this attempt to stabilize the year around a certain number of fixed moments, the sole elements of true history as the Church understood history, God's events reflected in human events and commemorated in feast days: Christmas cycle, Easter cycle, the great anniversaries and recurring pilgrimages. This was a kind of exalted history, put in order for all time, and lived out punctually by the faithful. But men, and facts, exceed this wondrous use of time in all directions. The year of history is like the year of a human life, and that is simply not the religious year, however rigorously it may try to conform. The year is not a uniform slice cut from the substance of time, any more than is the century. I do not claim that each year has its own unique dimension, density, and complexion. The year is no more than a frame, but in that frame a content takes place whose force and intensity are variable. In this sense, then, it can be said that there exist critical years, true focal points of events.

A look at modern history easily proves the point. It shows us how a given date may have its weight and value, with all the overlapping layers of time of which it is composed—and at the same time may serve as a point of observation (to stay within the metaphor I have used), offering the prospect of an extended area of history, of a large human landscape; the years 1793, 1830, and 1848 are examples. These are the great political dates, sharply defined by revolutions, the archetypal events. But that is something else again. These are the dates in the history of man, and in his intellectual and moral life—the peaks of certain generations. I am well aware that we tend to misuse those landmarks by clustering around them numerous data which may in point of fact precede or follow them. I am almost willing to admit that history is only very rarely its own contemporary in the absolute and rigorous sense—because, as I have shown, history is doubtless a superimposition of currents that differ widely in intensity, speed, and persistence. But, clearly, when we recall the man of 1848, and study the "focus" of the events through which he made his way, when we analyze his social, religious, economic, and intellectual life, we are dealing, not with a chronological fiction, but with positive and concrete data. It will be said that the man of 1848 is the same as the man of 1838 and 1858, and I am deeply convinced that this is true; but what gives him his place and defines him in the flow of time is that very year, understood both as a sudden conformation and as a millennial, a watershed. In the life of nations no less than of individuals, there are moments of heightened awareness and illumination, periods of paroxysm and of quickening. And there are also dates which we may regard as cardinal, the hinges on which we can in a sense see time turning.

It would of course be a grave error to regard history as a disparate collection of dates or spectacular years, but to interpret it as a monotonous sequence of facts would be equally erroneous. History is not a curve, nor is it a level plane—the profile it presents is most uneven. Our choice remains difficult and perilous; for whereas the unity—or apparent unity—of a human life justifies the principle and methods of biography, and whereas the study of the character and influence of a great work has a rational basis, it is a far more delicate undertaking to write the biography of a historical year, and first of all to choose it.

The era in which we are interested—so important in the history of the Europe it has shaped, and anything but a halfway house, or a sort of vague bridge leading from classical antiquity to modern times—does not lie before us as a homogeneous whole. On the contrary, it is greatly varied and highly structured, in point of geography as well as chronology. We can discern two great periods —the Germanic Middle Ages, and the Western Middle Ages. The Germanic Middle Ages are themselves quite complex: they open with the invasions, followed by the formation of barbarian political communities, and are climaxed by that masterpiece of fragility, their culmination and decisive expression, the Carolingian Empire. The Western Middle Ages, as I have attempted to show elsewhere, are a time when the West became aware of itself as the new guardian of culture, and a time of reaction against Germanism—either as a shapeless barbarity, or as barbarity organized.

Henri Pirenne, in his *Muhammad and Charlemagne*—a splendid book full of original and true and profound insights—makes the division differently. According to him, the Middle Ages in the strict sense begin on the day when the trade routes of the Western Mediterranean are cut off by Islam; the moment when Western Europe is compelled to live on its own substance and give up the economy of exchange; when the urban and Mediterranean character of its civilization gives way to a Nordic, rustic tenor. This is the deep mark which the Carolingians have left upon central and western Europe, and which will determine the future of those regions for centuries to come. The Carolingians mark the beginning of the Middle Ages. The era that precedes them is merely the last chapter in the history of the great Mediterranean civilizations. The Muslim invasion, closing the Mediterranean sea, threw Europe's culture back upon the North, and cut it off from that maritime hearth where, only the day before, it had found all its material and spiritual resources. The abundance of facts that Henri Pirenne advances, and the beauty of their presentation, would incline us to adopt the great historian's conclusions—if it were not that his work breaks off suddenly at the very moment when the question appears in a different light: the moment when out of the disintegration of the Carolingian Empire there begins to rise a new order.

But for a full understanding of the meaning of our search, we must return to its foundations. More than once we shall have occasion to do justice to Pirenne's remarkable work, right up to the point at which we are compelled to part company with him. Better than any other man, Pirenne has shown how insecure, precarious and, to say it bluntly, meager was the contribution made by those populations who, settled within the Roman Empire by choice or by force, grew prosperous in the Empire's disintegration to which they added a new ferment of their own. From the third century onward, the Empire is thrown on the defensive, although the vigor of the Illyrian emperors stands firm against marauders at the frontiers. The movements which arise at the end of the fourth century, and continue through the fifth, are of an entirely different magnitude. The populations in the path of those fearful pressures exerted by the vast hordes of nomads swarming out of the heart of central Asia must at all costs get into Romania—to find security, but most of all to find food. The texts cannot be made to yield anything even remotely resembling the theory of *Lebensraum*— the elements are different, the populations involved small in number; but the principle is the same: make room for us on pain of death, death for us or for you. Despite the disastrous nature of the results, we must admit the goodwill and even political wisdom of the emperors who, by various legal devices, received those populations into Roman territory; some were admitted as "guests," and allotted tracts of good land varying in size, others as "confederates" who received soldiers' pay turned over in a lump sum to their leaders, and thus became a body of auxiliary troops of the

Empire. These measures had been preceded, and were accompanied and no doubt encouraged, by what the ancient historians call barbarian infiltration. Their blood brothers held high offices in the civil or military administration; having become Roman citizens at heart and often in law, they would on occasion fight against the barbarians—but they could also offer them support. In this society luxurious in its habits, weakened in culture, divided and often rent asunder by political intrigue, a society whose fiber had grown softer, whose nerve was less vigorous than that of past generations—in such a society, the barbarians profited from the myth of the "primordial man," the noble savage alert to Nature's profound voices and adorned with the simple virtues: a myth we find in the texts from Tacitus to Salvian. As long as the confederates expressed their discontent—at payments overdue, subsidies slow in coming, the poor soil of their lands—by murmuring and sending delegations, and not by massacre, pillage, and arson, the Romans looked on them with neither surprise nor dislike; they regarded them, in Ferdinand Lot's words, as somewhat rude garrison troops.

The most remarkable fact is that the barbarians do not mingle with the population. Lot and Pirenne have established this fact beyond dispute. Even when they have set up kingdoms, they remain on the margins of Roman society, constituting what we would today call minorities. It may be that the relative smallness of their numbers compelled them to it; but it is also a constant characteristic of Germanic immigration. In most of the regions into which they move, even in modern times, the Germans remain clustered, forming a compact mass. We see it in the borderlands of Transylvania around Siebenbürgen, settled with Rhinelanders in the thirteenth century; in southern Russia; in southern Chile; and in certain districts of Brazil. We must add that, at the beginning of the Middle Ages, it is an absolute necessity for the chiefs to maintain the unity of their group with its own institutions, traditions, and spirit; it is an absolute necessity for them to forbid the *connubium*, a source of ethnic dissolution because children always follow the faith and education of their mother. So great is the prestige of the Empire and even of its ruins in western Europe, and so deep-rooted are the administrative and moral institutions of the old society, that the barbarian chiefs regard themselves for a long time as generals camped in friendly territory, or governors whose authority rests on delegation. The typical case is Theodoric, King of the Goths. He has been strongly marked, of course, by his Byzantine education; he is familiar at first hand with the system of Empire, and with the grandeur that it still retained in the East; and finally, the barbarian chieftain wields his power in an area whose society, more than any other, is the Roman society *par excellence*. And yet it may be stated in general that, despite differences in detail which are at times pronounced, the situation is the same in Frankish Gaul (excepting the extreme north) and Visigothic Spain.

This fact will help us understand why Romanism—I mean its tenor of life and principal forms of culture—has stayed alive and even prospered in the West of Europe, at least during the early stages of the growth of these political formations. Municipal administration continues to follow Roman patterns. Agriculture is practiced in the Roman manner. The Roman pound remains the standard of a lively commerce extending all around the Mediterranean, the still unbroken, still free area of the Old Empire, the unaltered zone of communication among all the Roman provinces now turned into separate kingdoms, which by the contiguity of their shores and by active trade maintain a geographic and economic unity. Even the local horizon of the Romans is not circumscribed by a wall: they furnish princes and bishops to the monarchies of the barbarians. Latin is the language not only of the chanceries, but also of trade and of daily life. It is the preeminent living language, and the language of the mind. It produces poets and writers—Sidonius Appolinaris, Fortunatus, Gregory of Tours among the Gauls, and Boethius, Symmachus, and Cassiodorus in Italy. Some of the barbarian princes have been not only men of letters but also masters of Latin oratory. Finally,

there is no break in the movement which had for so many generations fertilized the West with the contributions of the East. Syrian
and Jewish shipping enterprises connect the shores of Italy, Provence, Eastern Spain, and North Africa not only with Byzantium
but also with Egypt, Syria, and Anatolia. Now as in the past they
carry men and merchandise, monks and traders, fabrics and spices
and art objects. Nothing seems to have changed. The Roman
realm is not dead. It is differently structured, but its life seems to
rest upon the same foundations.

And yet something has changed profoundly. The barbarians,
side by side with the Romans who have become their masters,
evolve their own life in a totally different perspective. The central
fact, which can never be stressed too much, is that by their moral
status, their political organization, their instincts, and their art,
the barbarians belong to prehistory or, if you will, protohistory.
They have their own law, which, though written down in Latin,
has nothing Latin about it; on the contrary, it expresses an order
of human relationships which is diametrically opposed to the
ancient Roman idea of man and of society, a system of wergilds
and ordeals dating from the dawn of the ages. The morality of the
princes is unbridled; their annals are a long series of violent deeds,
assassinations, rapes, perjuries, and cruelties inflicted on the weak.
The Merovingian Gaul's idea of a king is the tribal chief or the
warlord, and not the magistrate or prince whose power, even if it
be absolute and tyrannical, is on all sides surrounded by a system
of laws or legal traditions, as it was in Rome. It is true, of course,
that the final centuries of the Empire have witnessed the onslaught
of military adventurers, the summary procedure of investiture by
acclamatio (though even this followed some sort of rules), as well
as frightful *coups d'état* and tragic palace revolutions. It is true,
of course, that the Imperial monarchy, through Eastern influence,
had gradually become a sort of theocratic despotism; yet through
all the periods of profoundest trouble the lawyers and the bureau-
crats, with their wealth of secular experience, preserved the idea
and tradition of the *res publica* that is totally alien to the barbarian

chieftains. When such a chieftain dies, his estate is divided up like booty, with no other rule or principle than to make all the lots roughly equal in value; towns separated by great distances may be thrown into the same lot simply to make it come out even. Just like primitive societies, the barbarian society has families of chiefs with the exclusive privilege to wield command, such as the Annals among the Goths, or the descendants of Merovech among the Franks. The dynastic principle and the rule of heredity, flagrantly opposed as they are to the principle of election, are in their essence prehistoric. Also prehistoric is the mode of life of these tribal chiefs, who maintain nomadic habits in traveling from one of their wooden palaces to another, and divide their time between war and the hunt. These habits were ingrained so deeply in the French monarchy that Louis XIV himself—accustomed to the vast forests around Paris, and as devoted to the hunt as were his forefathers, moving from Versailles to Fontainebleau, from Fontainebleau to Marly—may still, in this respect at least, be called a Merovingian prince.

Finally, the barbarians possess an art whose sources and character have given rise to much discussion. Its originality is no longer in doubt. It has undergone certain Mediterranean and, particularly, Oriental influences. But it is above all a degenerate form of a great protohistoric art of considerable complexity, whose traditions the Goths were able to acquire during their stay in southern Russia, the land of the Scythians and Sarmatians. The stylized animals characteristic of the art show an adaptation of the living form to the ornamental form, and combine, at least originally, two aesthetics which we wrongly treat as successive in order to fit them as much as possible into a chronological framework: the aesthetic based on the observation of nature, and that which concerns itself only with decorative values. The two go hand in hand since the Paleolithic Age. Be that as it may, the art of the Goths seems like a schematic hardening of these procedures, that of the Franks like an industrialized academicism, which mass-produces for a large clientele. The hopeless decline of the human figure which gives room to geometric combinations, the disappearance of stone sculpture which Bréhier has demonstrated, and the dominance of ornamentation which will henceforth overshadow all other forms of art—these are some of the unmistakable features of this chapter in our history. Building continued to follow models of that Mediterranean Latinity which is so marked by Eastern influences (we shall return to this point). But we are justified in the assertion that the architecture which has survived from the time of the barbarians—the crypts and baptistries of Gaul, for instance —reveals not so much the intrepid survival of the Roman spirit in an essential facet of its genius, as it reveals fatigue and senescence. This is the essential point. On funeral urns and screen plaques, on fibulae and belt buckles, the human figure, which in classical times was the center of gravity of the entire civilization, has been replaced by a prehistoric geometrism. The immediate prelude to the Middle Ages is—prehistory; later on, even the most original, most glorious creations of the Middle Ages will still bear the mark of the monotony of prehistory.

According to Pirenne, it was above all a popular art, crafted in Gaul by native artists—that is, Romans. On this basis, he proceeds to show how widely that art was diffused, and how much influence it had achieved at the expense of Mediterranean forms and techniques. Pirenne would have it that the princes had preserved a taste for art objects of the Mediterranean; yet this is not what the treasures of Tournai suggest—or those of Guarrazar, whose crowns decorated with pendants incontestably follow Cimmerian prototypes. We will have to admit that, from the top to the bottom of barbarian society, and including the "Romans" themselves, the moral structure of the populations of the Old Empire has been affected by the barbarian way and tenor of life, a certain way of looking at things, a certain manner of thinking. The Mediterranean is still open, but it cannot be denied that along its shores, where Latin is still spoken, new phenomena have appeared. The original status of the barbarians—the right of encampment or, if you will, life side by side—has changed by slow degrees. A hermetic seal between populations is a historical paradox, it is contrary to life. There has been interchange, if not fusion, a mutual penetration—and consequently a seesawing rise and fall: humanist culture sinking with the rise of the sumptuary arts, the ancient Latin forms giving way to an imitation orientalism, town life yielding to a semi-nomadic life, the idea of human dignity written in the law giving way to hierarchy based on conquest. In other words, history, the highest form of consciousness, gives way to prehistory. We must not mistake the enormous contribution of the barbarians; they brought with them decline—their own, their *Götterdämmerung*—and the decline of the Roman West. The most striking proof lies in the fact that the Eastern Empire, free of barbarian formations within, not only survived, but has added an indispensable page to the history of man.

A civilization is not defined exclusively by its elements, its characteristics, and its major features; it is defined above all by an altitude—the altitude of its view of life, its institutions, its thought, its art. Now, the altitude which Germanism forced upon the European West is exceedingly low, even though men still write Latin verse, even though honest and energetic shipmasters from the Levant still drop their cargo of spices on the piers of Marseilles. It will be said that Romanism could no longer survive; I do not know, nor does anyone else. In any case, Romanism did survive brilliantly in the eastern Mediterranean, where it maintained a great Empire and upheld a living tradition down to the middle of the fifteenth century. At the other end of Europe we find a weakening, senility. Deeds of violence and wars create an illusion of vitality in a society where we find two races living side by side, equally spent—the one perhaps by an excess of refinement, by the fatigue of a long history, and by political crises of unequaled magnitude, the other by the monotony of a crude culture without prospects, within which they had lived for centuries on the level of primitives. Such a race does not inject youthful and fresh strength, but a kind of crude and rustic mediocrity, a false vigor. We have only to read their chroniclers. *"Mundus senescit,"* one of them writes. The world is growing old—terrible words, expressive of a feeling that will darken men's hearts until the reawakening of the West. The last of the Merovingians in their ox carts are half asleep. The ultimate resource of Germanism is to double up a do-nothing monarchy, to respect its dynastic principle, by providing a head man who assumes the monarch's functions under the title of a mere domestic official, the Mayor of the Palace. But with its genius for anarchy, the German race sets Mayor against Mayor, just as in the past the petty kings collided in their quarrels over towns and abbeys. And yet, this very Mayoralty of the Palace, established by a *coup d'état* for the throne of the Frankish kings, and for the Lombard throne by right of conquest, brought about the resurrection of the Empire of the West. Did this resurrection draw support from that vague and pervasive nostalgia which later prompted the peoples to look back upon the imperial era as the golden age of human society? Surely not—and besides, in those days and circumstances the views of peoples had little effect on the conduct of public affairs. But we can be certain that the men of letters, the statesmen of Alcuin's type, did think of the matter, as did the educated clergy in the Lateran Palace surrounding a papacy grateful for Pepin's donation. We no longer hold with the doctrine which regarded the event of the year 800 as a master stroke of pontifical astuteness, but it is still true to say that the Romans of Rome and of Italy saw in this act of high politics a guarantee against the odious (and always possible) return of eastern heresies, and the resurgence of the Lombardian troubles. And the threat of Islam, master of the western Mediterranean—did it play a part in the matter? The texts tell us nothing.

Be that as it may, Charlemagne's Empire shows a remarkable internal contradiction. It is an attempt to restore Romanism in the administration and in the world of the academy, a "renaissance," artificial yet well organized, of the Roman spirit as it could be grasped in the writings of the ancient authors. This renaissance is at the same time profoundly Austrasian and Germanic. But does the closing of the Mediterranean to merchant shipping really

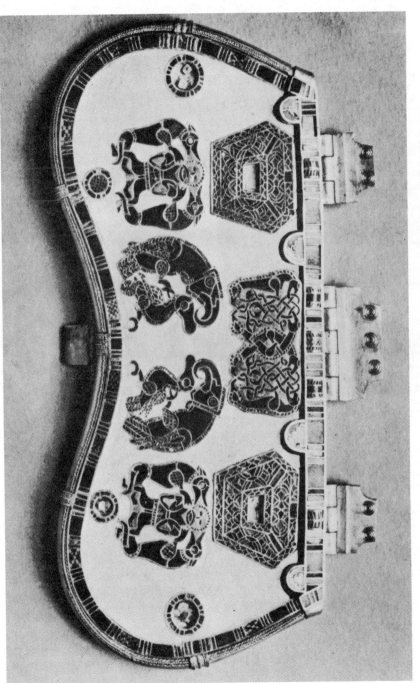

1. Purse lid, gold and enamel, from the Sutton Hoo (Suffolk) funeral bier. British Museum. Sixth-seventh century. (*Photograph*: British Museum.)

explain why Charlemagne establishes his capital, the center of his activities, in the North? We must not forget that the Pepinides have their origin in the Meuse region. In that region and in the Rhineland, they held those vast domains that were the foundation of their power as Mayors of Austrasia. Aix-la-Chapelle was, besides, the center of a political strategy which for a time would put an end to the old antagonism between the Germans of the West and the Germans of central Europe, between a more or less Romanized Francia and the Germania strictly speaking, which had remained altogether crude, primitive, and pagan in its forests, and constituted a threat as strong as the raids and piracies of the Muslim, and perhaps more frightful. We would thus be dealing with a natural result of the history of Germanism, rather than a side effect of the Islamic invasion. The same holds true, no doubt, for the rustic tenor of Carolingian life; its trade is exceedingly reduced, its industry truly manorial, the activity of its towns in deep decline. But is not the decadence of the towns a specifically Merovingian phenomenon? Ferdinand Lot's study of the town population seems decisive. It was no innovation when the Carolingians established the vast number of monasteries, those hybrid formations, half town, half manor, at least in the case of large abbeys such as Saint-Riquier and Saint-Gall. Underneath a structure of stronger, more centralized, more alert, and in a sense more "modern" administrative institutions, firmly supported by the prestige of the imperial title and the majesty of their titles from the chancery, the Carolingians perpetuate the barbarians. It can in fact be said that the balance, between what was left of Romanism in manners, culture, and the monuments of its culture, and the inferior level of the Germanic societies—that balance was not noticeably affected by the imperial restoration, nor by Islam establishing itself in the West.

What is this thing, a sea such as the Mediterranean? In itself, it is nothing but a watery waste, and also an open trade lane. What really matters are the countries along its shores. When the sea lanes are cut, are these countries totally isolated? Venice is still an open door toward the eastern Mediterranean and Byzantium, and what is more, the land routes remain free and much-traveled continental arteries. How else can we explain the numerous Mediterranean and Eastern elements found in the complex of Carolingian art? Italy continued to inspire certain typical forms present in Fulda, for example; and, if we are to accept Crosby's careful investigations at St. Denis, the circular crypt under the apse of the basilica built by Fulrad in the last third of the eighth century is essentially Latin, whereas the chapel added in the ninth century by Abbot Hilduin stands as one of the oldest examples in the West of those triple naves separated by unbroken walls which exist in Byzantine art and whose prototype Baltrusaitis found in Georgia. The church of Theodulf in Germigny-les-Prés is an Armenian church, related to the characteristic portion of the cathedral of Echmiadzin; and this is not an isolated case, since the same model can be found half a century later in the Asturias; there is thus reason to believe, with Puig i Cadafalch, that we are faced here with vestiges of a type generally adopted by Carolingian architects. The plan of two opposing apses is an ancient Latin plan, encountered again in Africa. Finally, how are we to explain that at the very moment when the West, in consequence of the closing of the Mediterranean, is supposed to become definitively Germanic and "Nordic"—that at that moment the representation of the human figure, side by side with lacework patterns, reappears in manuscript illuminations and begins to recover its lost splendor?

The question, then, seems to be more complex than it appeared at first. I do not believe that the Mediterranean saved Europe from barbarism in the centuries after the invasions and before the conquest of Islam. Nor do I believe that the closing of the Mediterranean made the Germanization of half of Europe inevitable. All in all, the situation of the Carolingian Empire at the beginning of the ninth century, with regard to the Mediterranean, is no worse than the situation of all of Europe in the second half of the fifteenth century. And the fall of the Byzantine Empire, which

2. **St.** Mark the Evangelist, from Irish Gospel. Codex 51, St. Gall Library. Eighth century. (*Photograph*: G. Micheli.)

turns the eastern Mediterranean into a Muslim lake, is certainly more serious than the loss of Spain in 711; the recovery of Spain becomes a certainty with the capture of Granada by the Catholic kings, but the incursions of the Barbary pirates in the western Mediterranean, where they continue to harass the Italian shores without let-up, remains a peril until Algiers is taken by the French in 1830.

In any event the Carolingian Empire, with its imperial and Roman façade, and its continuing contact with the old countries of ancient Romania and even the Near East, remains a powerful consolidation of Germanism for several generations at least. Did it place an indelible stamp on the European West, especially on France, Italy, and Germany? As concerns Germany, the point could hardly be denied. The Empire did so first of all by forcing Germany to enter Christian civilization, and lifting it through bloody wars out of its paganism and its chaos. It left Germany also with a deep psychological mark—an obsession with the universal Empire, a taste for boundless undertakings and colossal structures. We must never forget that Germany is a latecomer, dating only from the ninth century, that as a distinct political body she is still more recent, and finally that she enters into the life of Europe under the sign of the Empire which forced its forms upon her even before she had attempted autonomous experiments. Notwithstanding relapses into anarchy, she would long remain faithful to the principles on which she was originally organized and established. Here lies the explanation why Germany is slower, less original, and less creative than the other peoples involved in the general development of the great medieval civilization. At the height of the thirteenth century, Germany goes on building Carolingian basilicas; she is slow to adopt the Gothic style. She clings to her past everywhere. Feudalism survives untouched to the threshold of the modern age, perpetuating itself in a strong caste structure. Germany's greatness lies in her archaism. Her political function is twofold: she has a genuine function in her struggle against the Slavs and the peoples of the European northeast, and an artificial function in her forever vain attempts to get her hands on Italy and turn the Germanic Empire into a Holy Roman Empire, a universal power. The dismembering of Charles's inheritance has cut her off from the lands to the west, and the crowning of Otto I does not restore the tie. For a few generations, a powerful Austrasian family makes Germanic unity a reality. That family puts an end to the long wars which since Clovis's days had set the Christianized Germans settled on Roman territory against the barbarians of central Europe. The family dissolves in the tenth century—not only in political, but also in spiritual, terms. It is then—and not in the year 800—that the Middle Ages begin, as a reaction against Carolingian Germanism and the original definition of the West.

Considered geographically, the West is that part of Europe washed by the Atlantic and the North Sea. Its southern shores, in France and Spain, give it also a Mediterranean exposure, but the West faces horizons infinitely wider and more open, the icy seas toward the setting sun. So long as European civilization is more or less exclusively the work of Mediterranean peoples, it moves with wonderful assurance inside a narrow circle. It would be a mistake—still all too frequently committed—to think of the Mediterranean as a land-locked lake, a sort of Caspian Sea surrounded by a homogeneous territory. The Mediterranean is the meeting place and common ground of three continents—Europe, Africa, and Asia—and from this position it gains a wealth and intensity of elements that may explain, at least in part, the incomparable human quality of the great civilizations of antiquity. And yet, despite the caravans, the navigations, and mariners' reports, despite the extent of a commerce that reaches from Ophir to the Cassiterides, despite Alexander's Indian expedition, despite Agricola's campaigns in Great Britain—despite all this, the Mediterranean, marvelous crossroads, is a limit. The forces converging toward its center are more powerful than those radiating from it. Helped by a constant climate, gentle seasons, and the clearness of their skies, the peoples of the vine and olive tree—whose cultivation is an art—were able to achieve a historic success that has no equal; it may even be that if they had rolled back the frontiers of their world they would have endangered the true significance of their achievement. It is a good thing that, in their view, the river Okeanos formed an impassable barrier around the world. Those Phoenician sailors who dared to brave the dangers of the distant seas, pass beyond the Pillars of Hercules, and trace the coasts of the Dark Continent—did they add anything essential to civilization? It may be that the true inner meaning of the Punic Wars does not lie in the conflict between Rome and Carthage, between Latins and Semites, but rather in the large outlines of a dramatic encounter, between the purely Mediterranean idea of action—the idea of the lawyers, soldiers, wine-growers, and statuary sculptors on the one hand, and on the other hand a much larger and more diffuse idea such as befits merchants ceaselessly underway on the roads of the world. Besides, as soon as the limit shifts toward the East, and an excess of Asiatic thought penetrates first the Greeks' and then the Romans' thinking, the latter lose not just their purity but their vigor.

Be that as it may, there did exist around the happy sea, for some ten centuries, a most wonderfully arranged historic landscape, a choice territory for the highest development of human life. There is the possibility that, under different circumstances, it could have gone on lavishing its gifts indefinitely. That complex phenomenon called the Renaissance—which, incidentally, included so much of the Midde Ages—would incline us to believe in a new Mediterranean vocation; but it coincides exactly with vast discoveries overseas; and even without those discoveries, the tenor of European civilization had long since changed. The new landscape of civilization is not based in central Europe. One look at a map will make the point clear. The old continental dominion of the Germans, bordered by the Alps, the Rhine, the Baltic, and the Slavic countries, and without any natural connection with the Atlantic or the Mediterranean, seems condemned to a kind of vast provincialism, a life that is sluggish and frantic by turns. A history of Germany's development must be mindful not only of the fact that her entry into the European community came late, but also of her unusual geographical position in Europe, dating from the treaty of Verdun. Germany has an imperial outlook because she arose in violence out of the Carolingian wars and the Carolingian Empire. She bears the marks of the iron that attended her birth in pain and anguish. From prehistory she has preserved the instinct of war to the finish, the nostalgia of the forests and of the migration of nations, the belief in the absolute value of an over-population pressing upon the neighboring tribes. She sends abroad large colonies, which religiously maintain the provincial tenor of their origins. Her indifferent vista upon a sea of shallow waters, the Baltic, make her the least ventilated section of Europe. It is only natural that she should pursue racial dreams, and seek escape in philosophy and music, the fields in which she shows such greatness, and finally that she should look upon the universe with greed rather than human curiosity. These observations are not meant to 'reduce systematically the contributions and merits of a nation, but to explain, in the light of established facts drawn from history and geopolitics, why the Germanic complex in the strict sense, important as it is in the Middle Ages, has neither produced the Middle Ages no reven colored them. The essential experiments of the Middle Ages did not occur in Germany, nor in the Mediterranean.

History is made of a threefold cluster of activating forces—traditions, influences, and experiments; and every civilization, perhaps every epoch of every civilization, stresses one or the other of these forces in turn. Tradition resembles a vertical force rising out of the depth of the ages; but at times it loses its cohesion, its vital drive (though it is not completely broken), and then fictions and distorting myths appear in its place. Perhaps this must be so if tradition is to adapt itself to the new times. Tradition is only seldom unalloyed. In fact, there are traditions that are out and out inventions, to serve this or that cause, and they are of no small interest. But diverse as the facets of tradition's internal ferment may be, the ferment represents the working of the past in the historical present. Influences, in turn, represent the technique of interchange and cross-fertilization. Peoples communicate with other peoples by such influences; the foreign contributions which they bring are accepted more or less passively—by way of infiltration, or by a shock, because they answer a profound need or because they are disturbing. They are like a horizontal level of water rippled by diverse currents which establish a kind of changing harmony, a more or less stable consensus within the human community. But the enrichment and renewal of history clearly come from the experiments that are quickened by man's urge to inquire and create. Experiments, one might say, dig into the future. They may be groping, insecure, and full of mistakes; they may not always be fortunate; but without them the substance of history would quickly be exhausted, without them there would be no history but merely a hopeless round of lifeless forms of conservatism. Periods bereft of the genius of trial and of risk lend truth to the brief and terrible phrase of the Merovingian writer, *mundus senescit*. The Middle Ages developed in opposition to this senescence, this senility; and the source of the experiments that gave the Middle Ages not merely their grandeur but their inexhaustible capacity for youthful vigor is the West, the lands of the West.

The lands are Norway and its Scandinavian "tenants," sailors of the vast oceans on which their country itself seems to float; and the British Isles, Gaul, and Spain. The last two enjoy the advantage of facing in two directions, toward the Atlantic and the Mediterranean. But from the seventh century onward, Spain is overcast by Islam. Her historic labor, before the discovery and colonization of the great Indies, has two sides: first the reconquest of the Christian territories, and then the transmission to the West of those elements of Muslim culture which can be assimilated. Beginning in the tenth century, Spain's northeasterly part, the old "Spanish province" with its highly developed culture—a region that Charlemagne had driven into the Muslim orbit—produces constructive experiments of great importance to the future of the Middle Ages; but what it contributes is essentially Mediterranean. For long periods, its ungenerous soil, one of Europe's oldest geological formations, is a kind of Africa where three cultures are grappling with each other; its intellectual life and the monuments of its culture testify to this. There is an oriental culture, displaying its loveliest gifts and creating a first form of medieval humanism in the harmony of Muslim, Greek, and Jewish thought; there is an ancient Mediterranean culture, producing polished Latinists and the builders of the vaults in the monasteries of Catalonia; and finally there is the culture which is properly Western, brought in first by Cluny, then by Cîteaux, then by the builders of the great cathedrals—a culture leading to the renewed flowering on Spanish soil of the churches of Aquitaine, then of Burgundy and the royal domain. But what is most remarkable is that these cultures, diverse as they are, do not just exist side by side, nor are they content to follow one another like the stage settings of a play in several acts. They exchange their resources and produce experimental hybrids of strange beauty: a Roman art of Islam—the Mozarabic art—and an Islamized Gothic art, the art of the *Mudejares*. As we study the Mozarabic churches of the tenth century, under the guidance of Gomez Moreno, we are stunned by their variety and inventive power, notwithstanding the continuity of their specific liturgical structure and spirit. Although the Arabs left a deep imprint, although the North contributed a large share, Spain created a tone and quality in her architecture, and in her people, which are entirely her own. Equipped with the many elements produced by the extraordinary clash of peoples on the Spanish scene, Spain strikes out on a search which is and always will remain original. It is true, of course, that at that point in time at which we see her, her Atlantic vocation has not yet declared itself; but once she has put an end to her internal struggle, between North and South, or more precisely between the Mediterranean West and Africa, she embarks on the ocean lanes with a driving energy well known to us, to set up a new world under distant skies.

3. St. Mark the Evangelist, from Ebbon's Gospel. Manuscript 1722, Epernay Library.
Ninth century. (*Photograph*: Archives Photographiques.)

Gaul of the High Middle Ages is twofold, despite her territorial and human homogeneity. Neustria and Austrasia represent not just two different political configurations but two facets of her genius. The struggle of the Neustrian Mayors of the Palace against those of Austrasia has for the moment been decided in favor of the latter; it may even be said that the foundation of the Carolingian Empire is the result—and the greatest achievement—of Austrasian politics. But the whole historical future of the third race has its focus and center of expansion in the royal domain, abutting on the maritime regions. The historic function of Paris is largely defined by the activities of the sailors plying the waters of the upper and lower Seine. The Paris region is one of the most important, perhaps the most important, crossroads of the waterways of western Europe. In this region, not far from the Channel, modern France had her beginnings; from here she launched her long struggle to regain direct access to the sea, and to recover the territories which Charles the Simple ceded to the Normans at the beginning of the tenth century. In the sixth century, Brittany had been settled by people from Wales and Cornwall fleeing the Germanic invasions of Great Britain; this ancient massif of granite, bristling with megalithic monuments, the farthest outpost of the West jutting out into the ocean, maintained its contact with the Isles through fishing, trade, and war, faithful to the maritime mission that geography had imposed on it—a mission it had embraced since the Gallic wars, when Caesar wrote of the fleet of the Veneti, with their heavy vessels steered by means of devices made of iron. South of the Loire stretches a long coastline, the border of one of the most active and most prosperous regions in the Middle Ages—Poitou, Saintonge and, in a general way, Aquitaine; the southern part of Aquitaine might well be called the land between two oceans, since it touches on the Atlantic as well as on the Mediterranean. While Brittany remains apart for a long time, closed to all except Norman influences, the historic monuments of the southwest bear witness to the extreme variety of its history; in the Romanesque period, the strong imprint left by Roman builders is still visible in the use of beautiful columns placed against the façades or in the apses; the architecture of the vaults is Mediterranean; and the treatment of decorative sculpture recalls the Arab ivories, or chests covered with hunting scenes brought back from the Spanish crusade. All these impress upon us how fruitful were the contacts in the West, especially in France by virtue of her exposure in two directions—and also in Spain, though France enjoyed the advantage of remaining Christian territory, a free country.

We cannot deny for an instant the Mediterranean origins of Romanesque architecture; nor may we underrate the part that the Muslim withdrawal played in introducing certain Near Eastern elements to the Gauls. It is valuable to know that the Arabs lost their base of Garde-Freinet in 973, and that the Pisans, at the beginning of the eleventh century, were beginning to sweep the western Mediterranean. We mention another coincidence, or rather a simultaneous event of no small interest: At that same time, the Bagratid princes, the great builders of churches whose influence is noticeable in Gallic architecture and sculpture, were liberating the Armenian region. Those monuments, however, do not travel in numbered crates in the holds of well-guarded vessels. The matter is more complex and more subtle. It may in fact be stated that all passive imitation, just as all importation, is well-nigh fruitless unless it falls on fertile soil, among a people who take it up, rethink it, and reshape it in keeping with their own needs. To stress the astounding variety of French Romanesque art is utterly useless; it has long been studied in terms of "schools," a hoary term which yet has the merit of underlining the great variety of experiments and wealth of solutions. Even within a highly homogeneous group, such as the basilicas along the pilgrims' roads, we find profound differences among such churches as those of St. Martial in Limoges, Sainte-Foy in Conques, and St. Sernin in Toulouse. But the experimental character and inventive power stand out when we compare a Burgundian church of the Cluniac type with another, in the same region, of the Vézelay type—and even more when we go from Normandy to Provence, or from the southwest to Auvergne. While the colossal churches on the Rhine, those splendid Carolingian mastodons, seem witnesses of a defunct art stranded on the sands of time, the Romanesque art of the West is alive with the intensity and variety of inexhaustible resources. We gain an even stronger sense of this if we take a position at the beginnings of this development, and watch how it is born in the ninth century, and how it defines itself more and more precisely in its quest, through trials which start with a suggestion received from a distant prototype and arrive at the creation of new forms.

Thus the experiment of the West is a highly original reflection of Mediterranean sources. The oriental element that pervades Romanesque sculpture is employed according to an architectural and human logic which is wholly our own. More compellingly, Gothic art stands before us as an experiment that is thoroughly Western. It has been shown, of course, that there are Armenian ogives which have been imitated in literal detail in Italy, and in certain military structures in France. True, there are examples of ancient Lombard ogives which may be related to methods used by the Romans. But Gothic art has nothing Mediterranean about it. Its essential technical features were tried out variously in more than one French region, and it achieves its status as a systematic and new form of the building art in Normandy and England—at Lessay, in St. Paul's in Rouen, at Durham (1093–1104). Finally, the region in which it gives birth to a style, which means a coherent, original, and complete system, is the heart of Francia, the Île de France; this is done through a series of experiments following each other in such rigorous sequence that they have been compared to the consecutive steps in the demonstration of a theorem. Even German scholars have been compelled to give up the notion that this art is of German origin, since Germany was, of all nations, most slow to adopt it. To interpret it as a dream of the Germanic races about nature and the divinity is an old romantic fiction; the rationality, the harmony, and the measured control informing the most daring combinations of the *opus francigenum* have done away with German influence beyond recall.

Gothic art, then, is the pure expression of a Western idea and quest. Considering their birthplace, it could even be said that this idea and this quest belong essentially to Atlantic civilization. The economic ties linking Great Britain to France, the road that leads from Boulogne through Noyon to the trading towns of the Champagne, have given the Gothic soil of the West a new and notable coloring; their influence adds to the effects produced, during the immediately preceding period, by the political relations between Normandy and England.

But the British contribution of original elements to the emergence of the Western genius dates from more ancient times—not from Southern England, where Augustine's missionary action introduced Christianity in the Roman fashion, but from Northumberland, Scotland, and above all Ireland. In its remote Celtic setting, Ireland had preserved rich deposits from the civilization of the Bronze Age: it is astonishing to witness, after fifteen centuries of slumber, the vigorous and abundant resurgence of spiral and lacework, while Irish Christianity develops its own tonality, engages in those famous controversies to strive to preserve its own understanding of the liturgy, and produces a hagiography full of miracles mingled with fragments of prehistoric epics. Irish culture doubtless received many gifts from the Mediterranean, as for example the contributions of the Coptic monks of certain monasteries; but there can be no doubt that Ireland, out there in the Atlantic, represents a center of great antiquity and originality, a kind of maritime Celtism whose ways of thinking and inquiry run counter to classical humanism, not by chance or by whim, but by virtue of a turn of mind which is neither Mediterranean nor Germanic. Ireland surely made the most daring experiments using the human form as an ornamental motif, in the leaf-shaped men and lacework men of the old breviaries. From Ireland came not only St. Columban, the founder of Luxeuil and Bobbio, but also those *peregrini Scotti*, pilgrims to all of Western Christendom, who

4. Altar frontal from the chapel, Aachen (Aix-la-Chapelle). Around 1000. (*Photograph:* Marburg.)

everywhere taught their strange secrets, the magic of line combinations; they were so successful that Carolingian miniatures—bound between covers that are still decorated with uncut precious stones in the manner of barbarian goldsmiths—exhibit side by side a renaissance of the human figure in accordance with Mediterranean principles, and amazing abstract gardens and flowerbeds of lacework where pure form is its own delight, offering infinite opportunities to all the whims of the imagination. The revival of some of these old forms, and in particular of the *contre-courbe*, at the beginning of the fourteenth century, will make their contribution to the flamboyant style. In matters other than decor, what is there in common, for example, between the tall and slender towers of Glendalough, standing like stone candles, and the massive Carolingian architecture? Though certain Carolingian ivories in the reliefs which adorn the Irish crosses shown in Françoise Henry's book [1] might have been copied, it is not they that give character to those monuments—far from it—but rather the ancient sun disk combined with the crucifix, the panels of lacework, the hunting and fighting scenes carved on the socles, scenes borrowed from the ancient epic poetry of the island. This is the milieu from which arises the strangest and perhaps most profound thinker of the entire Middle Ages, Scotus Erigena, whose visionary theology, so rich in metaphysical substance, constitutes in the ninth century a lively contrast to the academicism of Byzantine thought and its empty quarrels.

The Scandinavians prompt other reflections. We forget too easily that there are two kinds of Germans: those of the continent, and the people of the sea. The continental Germans found their home grounds long ago in the region of central Europe which now bears their name; after the partition of the Carolingian Empire, but even more after the founding of the Holy Roman Empire of the German Nation, their main energies turn eastward against

[1] F. Henry, *La sculpture irlandaise dans les douze premiers siècles de l'ère chrétienne*, Paris, 1933.

the Slavs, and southward against Italy. The others, the Normans, spread their incursions over vast areas, mainly in the Atlantic, until the great age of the Vikings, when Canute founds an empire that swallows England; and England awaits her final conquest by another Viking whose forefathers, a century and a half earlier, had become vassals of France—William the Conqueror. These two kinds differ not only in the directions of their migrations, the Normans went as far as southern Italy and Sicily, but in the characteristics of their culture. If the continental Germans have ever had any originality, it is certain that by the ninth and tenth centuries they had completely lost it; the complex of Carolingian civilization, which anyway was wholly artificial, is in essence Mediterranean, although there are some Irish contributions and barbarian survivals. By contrast, those same centuries are the era of the greatest splendor of Scandinavian culture, from the steles of Gotland to the war ships of Vestfold. We cannot here discuss the difficult question of the Scandinavians' relationship with the civilization of the British Isles, or with Ireland; for our inquiry it does not matter what they gave, or what they took. They have not, by the way, been without influence on the continental West. We need not recall the enormous jambs of Bayeux. But neither must we overestimate these contributions. The theory whereby Gothic art is indebted for certain fundamentals to the wooden churches of Norway rests on a chronological interpretation which is more than questionable, and on an incorrect assimilation of wooden construction to construction in stone. No—the important thing is that we are dealing in these regions with a culture of extraordinary drive and vitality, a culture which, upon a foundation of the monotony of certain prehistoric themes, multiplied its creative experiments, renewed the style of animal portrayal, and gave proof of a wealth of skills which it had already demonstrated by its remarkable achievements in the Bronze Age. The greatness of Germania must be sought here, in the lands rendered fertile by the sea, the last outpost of Western man toward the icy pole. From these shores it set out, pushing toward the distant west, to Greenland, to the continent of America, long before the age of the great discoveries.

It is notable, though not surprising, that the Christianization of Scandinavia should little by little neutralize this originality, and that the art of the Mediterranean, in its Romanesque form, would finally drive out those charming and bizarre lacework portals that represent the final stage, the baroque stage of Scandinavian culture. This is only one aspect of the conflict which, in the drama of the Middle Ages, sets the Mediterranean against the Atlantic, the peoples of the West against the peoples of central Europe, the continental Germans against the Germans of the sea. We have seen some of its episodes—the position of the barbarians with regard to the great historical constructions of the Mediterranean, the creation of Germany by the Carolingians and the mark they have left on her, and finally the awakening of the West to make its own experiments—not by breaking its ties with the Mediterranean but rather by defining a new site, a new landscape for human civilization. In essence, the Middle Ages are neither Mediterranean nor Germanic nor "Nordic." They are Western. They have built not only churches, but a society. In the place of the piled-up ruins of the fallen Carolingian Empire, and the feudalism grown out of its decay (and which is exactly the state of primitive organizations that are still found in Black Africa at the end of the nineteenth century), the Middle Ages strained to establish a new order—by the Magna Charta, by the franchising of the towns, by the century-long efforts of the Capetian kings to destroy other feudal lords and give France that profound unity, that character of a modern nation which Germany and Italy have attained only recently. The West, fronting on the Atlantic, is the foundation of the civilization of the Middle Ages and of modern times, as Greece, washed by the waves of the Mediterranean, is the foundation of the civilization of antiquity.

I am stressing these facts, but not in order to surround the year 1000 with useless reflections. It is simply that this year seemed to me one of those in which the Middle Ages expressed themselves with full vigor. We shall see the events which then took place within Islam, with the decline of the caliphate of Cordova; in Scandinavia, with decisive wars and the conversion to Christianity; in the Empire and in Rome, where Gerbert and Otto III establish an extremely precarious universal monarchy, a symbol of the weakness of Germany's Italian ambitions; and finally in eastern Europe, where the Hungarians, who for so long had devastated the West, become at last its defenders and serve as an outpost of the apostolic monarchy against the barbarians of the steppes. Elsewhere, the churches of the same period, with their strong continuity of Carolingian architecture in the north of France, will demonstrate to us the perfection and wide dispersion of certain Mediterranean types of a form which is very ancient but amenable to revolutionary new applications—the vault—while in France's center, the Loire region, there is rapidly developing a new type of apse which is destined to become a characteristic element of Western architecture in the Romanesque and the Gothic age. Traditions, influences, and experiments combine: the West, the Mediterranean, and the East work hand in hand. We still need to identify the part each of them plays. We still need to study and portray, against a background which is as yet obscure, certain figures whose profile is anything but negligible. For history consists not only of currents, events, and settings—history consists essentially of human values.

5. Apocalypse, from St. Millan de la Cogolla. Manuscript 33, Academy of History, Madrid. End of tenth century. (*Photograph*: from D. Bordona, *Exposicion de codices miniados españoles*, 1929.)

ONE

The Problem of the Terrors

BY what right do we introduce phenomena of collective psychology into the study of history? They certainly are most difficult to grasp with any degree of precision. We have immediate comprehension of the meaning and life of an institution, the causes and effects of a military action or a political treaty. We even can reconstitute the variables that have affected a human mind. But we are much less equipped to enter the vast undefined realm of instincts, or of the beliefs and undercurrents that move not individuals but crowds. Yet how can we ignore this element when we are dealing, for example, with religious faith, or with a revolutionary faith? To disregard such basic sociological matter would be extremely dangerous, even though it may, and often does, assume a fantastic character. Those great waves of emotion, love, and fear that stir up a whole people are not necessarily romantic illusions. What must be done is first to demonstrate their presence in the texts, to study them, and to show their relative depth and intensity at various times and in various places.

As we set out to study a crucial year in the history of the West, it would perhaps be more prudent first to lay a firm foundation for it, rather than enter by this difficult and uncertain door. Yet, although serious historians have expressed the most emphatic reserve concerning the terrors of the year 1000, the two ideas—the year 1000, and the terrors—remain firmly associated in minds of sound intelligence, especially among certain archaeologists. This association is not just the outgrowth of a romantic view of the Middle Ages which belongs to the nineteenth century. It allows a convenient classification of the facts: In the year 1000, the West reaches the peak of those misfortunes that had beset it throughout the tenth century; the belief in the end of the world is reawakened by the approach of the fateful date, and nourished by signs and wonders; a nameless fear grips all mankind; the time which the apostles prophesied has come. . . . But the year passes, the world is not destroyed, mankind breathes relief and gratefully sets out on a new road. All things are changed, all things improve— first of all religious architecture. In a famous text to which we shall return, the monk Glaber writes: "About three years after the year 1000, the world put on the pure white robe of churches." [1]

Certain recent historians have yielded to the temptation to paint the portrait of this period of the Middle Ages in clashing colors, laying on deep shadows and bright hues by turns, and have humored their talent by stressing the convulsive nature of the crisis. Does this mean that we, having dispelled the legend of the terrors, must now concern ourselves exclusively with the constructive events that are remarkable during this period, and, filled with optimism, represent the age as after all one of the happy moments in the history of man? Or, as some writers have done, must we adopt a prudent position in the middle, equidistant from both excesses, and somehow neutralize the year 1000, making of it a year like all the others, one among many?

The question is more complex. We must first solve the problem of the terrors and calamities, taking into account a number of facts. It is not meaningless to speak of the beliefs of millenarianism. What is their origin, their—vastly different—development in the East and in the West, what their significance in the evolu-

[1] Raoul Glaber, *Les cinq livres de ses histoires* (900–1044), ed. M. Prou, Paris, 1866, III, Ch. 4; E. Pognon, *L' an mille*, Paris, 1947, p. 89.

tion of Christian thought? Did they not have an effect, at some moment in the tenth century, in certain regions and among certain classes? What may have been the role of the revival of apocalyptic studies? How did it happen that the terrors were assigned to the year 1000—which at first appears altogether natural, but is incorrect? Finally, what is their place in the archaeological study of the Middle Ages? Only when we have answered these questions can we proceed to the objective analysis of our subject.

I

The idea of the end of the world is known to almost all the ancient peoples, as a basic element of their religion or philosophy, as are the ideas of a glorious rebirth and thousand-year cycles. In Iranian Mazdaism, winter and night will cover the world at the end of eleven thousand years; but the resurrected dead come down from the kingdom of Yima to repopulate the earth. Analogous beliefs are found in Germanic mythology, and in certain Islamic communities. The philosophies of Heraclitus and of the Stoa were already more or less imbued with parallel doctrines. Cicero, in his *On the Nature of the Gods*, explains that the world will end in fire—but since fire is spirit, that is, divine, the world will be reborn as beautiful as ever.

According to Christian millenarianism, Christ will return to rule the earth for a period of a thousand years—the Latin *millenium*, Greek *chiliasm*. The idea is essential to primitive Christianity, the continuation of an ancient Judaic tradition. Harnack [2] has well described the development of the idea and the complexity of its component elements: the supreme battle against the enemies of God, the return of Christ, the Last Judgment, and the establishment of a glorious kingdom on earth. In Jewish apocalyptic literature—Jeremiah, Ezekiel, Daniel, and the Psalms—the duration of the messianic kingdom is not limited. Then a new idea is born: a distinction is made between the coming of the Messiah

[2] Adolf Harnack, article *Millenium* in Encyclopedia Britannica, 1934.

and the appearance of God the Judge. From this distinction follows the limited duration of the Messiah's kingship in the strict sense. Baruch calls it limited but does not specify its duration—according to him it will last until the corruption of the world comes to an end; his text is very valuable to us, because it keeps us from confusing the messianic kingdom, in which mankind is still struggling against sin, with the kingdom of glory. In the apocalypse of Ezra, and in the Talmud, the time span of the messianic kingdom is four hundred years. But the duration given most often is a thousand years—a day for God, a day of a thousand years. In the Middle Ages we witness the re-emergence of this idea of an enormous week, whose seven days constitute the seven ages of the world; the last age, occupied by the messianic kingdom, has the significance of a Sabbath. Harnack rightly points out that the principle of limited duration appears nowhere in the gospels, nor in the apostolic writings. But the Apocalypse of St. John, this strange testimony to the survival of Jewish thought among the Asiatic Christians, is specific: the messianic kingdom will last a thousand years. Then Satan will return for a short time, and he will be destroyed. The dead will rise from their graves to be judged, and—as in Mazdaism—a new universe, a kingdom of glory, will be created for the elect. Eusebius reports that a Judeo-Christian, Cerinthus, envisioned the new universe filled with oriental sensuality: after the apocalypse of destruction and punishment, the apocalypse of human delights. Be that as it may, henceforth the idea is in its large outlines orthodox, in one form or another; and the doctors who attempt to reconcile paganism and Christianity —for instance, Justin—retain it as an essential element of the latter.

Our period may be said to have seen the greatest flowering of millenarian ideas. John's Apocalypse, both flaming and obscure, despite all differences of interpretation, nevertheless stimulated this feeling of suspense, this faith on the alert, full of expectancy, which is peculiar to the messianic hope. The Lord had come. The Lord would return. The Lord would judge the living and the dead.

6. The Last Judgment, from Henry II's Epistle. Latin manuscript 4452, Munich Library. Early eleventh century. (Photograph from G. Leidinger, *Miniaturen der Staatsbibliotek München*, 1911.)

How to compute the time when it would happen? That tremendous day, the last day and last age of the world—was mankind even now immersed in it, would it end, would the Antichrist soon make his appearance? The controversy between the literal and the mystical interpretations starts in the middle of the second century. The old Jewish millennium falls into disrepute, having been adopted by Montanism. The Greek church grows more and more distrustful of what it conceives to be a visionary's dream, to the point of excluding the Apocalypse from the canonical writings. Attempts at conciliation, such as that of Dionysius of Alexandria, alleviate only temporarily a dispute over the issue of the millennium; within Christianity, this dispute pits the Jewish genius against the Greek genius, the trembling hope of eternal messianism against Hellenistic mysticism. The theologians of Alexandria and Byzantium banish the Apocalypse, while the old communities of the East, more or less steeped in Judaism, retain it. One might ascribe the phenomenon to a narrow traditionalism cropping up in closely circumscribed quarters—Coptic Egypt, Arabia, Ethiopia—if it were not that the West, whose theology is so alive and rich, shows the same conservatism in master theologians like Tertullian, Lactantius, and Sulpicius Severus. We notice with amazement not just a simple difference in tone but a conflict in doctrine.

The former camp does not doubt in the least the authenticity and apostolic character of John. It does not in the least doubt the future or the imminent coming of the Christ who will establish his earthly kingdom and the Church of the Saints for a thousand years. It does not in the least doubt the return of Nero as the Antichrist. It would not be too much to say that apocalyptic millenarianism with its powerful visualizations, its Judaic speculations on numbers, and its gasping vagueness concerning the moment when the days will be accomplished, maintains the Church in this state of dramatic alarm which is so suitable to the oriental Christians and so repugnant to Christian Hellenism.

Could it be that the influence of the Greek Fathers, making itself felt through scholars such as St. Jerome, finally came to weaken and to still the apocalyptic faiths? Are we confronted here with a collapse such as often follows after the high moral tension and youthful virulence of a doctrine? Is it, finally, the interpretation of the millennium by St. Augustine, who seems to end the terror in the Christian soul, or rather to appease it, by extending the millennium over centuries? For Augustine, the Church is the kingdom of Jesus Christ, and the millennium began in the year of the Incarnation. In a meaty and most welcome article, Émile Gebhart[3] presents the problem in a wholly different manner. He assumes that the bishop of Hippo, who witnessed the downfall of the Empire, believed himself a spectator at the first act of the drama that Daniel had envisioned, St. John foretold, and St. Paul affirmed—the duel between Antichrist and Jesus in which Jesus will at first seem vanquished. The final act will come only after a thousand years of temporal rule by the Church of Christ. The downfall of the Empire, Gebhart adds, is merely the "obligatory prologue" of the millennium; one must add at least four hundred years to the period of which Augustine himself had not seen the dawn. This theory of an "obligatory prologue" of four hundred years is in fact highly debatable. If the Augustinian millennium, the earthly reign of Christ, begins with the Christian Church, its beginning must obviously coincide with the birth of Jesus. If pressed, we might accept Constantine's official recognition of Christianity as the starting point—but not the fall of the Empire which, anyway, extends through several generations and is not strictly speaking a "date." Glaber, who gives the year 1000 as the end of the millennium, does not deserve Gebhart's criticism, because he is right. It will be said, of course, that it is a strange, earthly kingship of Christ that rules over a world so full of sin and crime. True—but Baruch's Apocalypse had given us warning: *Donec finiatur corruptio mundi.* The militant Church, then, works in the midst of

[3] E. Gebhart, "L'état d'âme d'un moine de l'an mil," *Revue des Deux Mondes,* September 1891, pp. 600ff.; *Moines et papes, essais de psychologie historique. Un moine de l'an 1000,* etc., Paris, 1896. See also E. Pognon, *L'an mille,* Paris, 1947, pp. 41ff.

a corruption which it is trying to end—until that day, after Satan's final convulsion, after the universal Judgment, when the Church Triumphant, the Church of God's communion, will be raised up in a renewed world. The earthly reign is thus not the reign of virtue and peace, but the unfolding of the drama of fall and redemption, a drama filled with catastrophe and ruin.

Thus after Augustine millenarianism seems to have disappeared from the official doctrine of the Church in the West, and in the end that Church adopted the views of the Greek Fathers, but there were certain areas of religious thought where it preserved a strange vitality. It might be thought that there exists a violent contradiction between the humanism of the gospels, which gives peace, and apocalyptic Judiasm, which gives alarm. In reality, each of the two satisfies certain needs of the human soul, and it may even be said that they complement each other. A society that is deeply troubled and often unhappy, naturally tends to read literally the great texts from which millenarianism has arisen; but even more generally, it tends to give an apocalyptic interpretation to history, to worship the God of Terror, and to live in the expectation of Judgment Day. When will that Judgment take place? A thousand years after the Incarnation, or fourteen hundred years? No—but tomorrow morning, because tonight I may die, and from that moment on my fate is sealed. How long one waits in the night of the tomb is of no matter, because by then it will be too late to alter the sentence of the Supreme Judge. The Apocalypse cries out to me to be ready, and the frightful misery of the world is nothing, after all, compared with the scourges that will announce its end.

This is why the Western Middle Ages, millenarian or not, kept reading the Revelations of St. John and even the Apocalypses of Ezra and of Hermas which are included in certain Bibles. This is why the commentaries and the illustrations of John's Apocalypse have played so large a part in the spiritual life of the Middle Ages. The commentaries of Victorinus were followed by many others. St. Caesarius composed no less than nineteen homilies on the work of St. John, and the Blessed Ambrose Antpert devoted ten books to it. In this line of great interpreters belong Beatus of Liebana; Haimon of Halberstadt; Berengar of Ferrière; and Rémi, monk of St. Germain of Auxerre—all of them investigators of the mysterious book. Beatus—St. Beatus—most deserves our attention because his commentary has had a deep and enduring influence on the thought and art of the Middle Ages of the Romanesque period. We have some interesting biographical data about him. Born around 730 and deceased in 798, he was the spiritual director of Queen Osinda, wife of Silo king of Oviedo (771–783). He thus seems representative of that Christian culture which the petty princes of the Asturias, of Visigothic strain, did their part to maintain in northern Spain. As the abbot of Liebana, he belongs to that Mozarabic Christianity which was influenced by Islam which was one of the curious hybrids of Iberian civilization. He would have been one of the teachers of Alcuin and Emerius of Osma. But he is first of all the author of the Commentary on the Apocalypse, which dates from 776. At first it appears that the doctrinal import of this work is limited to a theological controversy on points of dogma which had troubled and were still troubling the Greek Church, concerning the nature of the Son and of the Father. It played a major part in the struggle against Felix of Urgel and Elipando of Toledo, partisans of Adoptionism, the heresy according to which the Son and the Father are not consubstantial because the Son had been chosen, *adopted* by the Father for his perfection.[4] But the human horizon encompassed by St. Beatus' *Commentary* is much larger, by virtue of the astounding illustrations with which it has been embellished in the *scriptoria* of the Mozarabic monasteries. Besides the painting of the monuments of that Islamized Christianity which are shown there as the seven churches of the Apocalypse, we have a picture of the last days of the world that does justice to the majestic horror of the catastro-

[4] On Beatus of Liebana and Adoptionism, see E. Amann, *Histoire de l'Eglise*, Vol. 6, "Epoque carolingienne," Paris, 1947, pp. 130ff. (with bibliography). The writings of Beatus have been published by Florez, Madrid, 1770.

phe, and is made to strike men's imagination with supreme conviction. In addition, the illustrations possess the unique individuality of a kind of western orientalism, enhanced here by the attraction of the garish and yet sweet colors in combinations peculiar to Islamic art. The texts are meant for those who can read, the illustrations of these admirable books for those who cannot read; and the same holds true even more when the illustrations are transferred to the stone of the basilicas. We must never forget that, apart from the clerics, the culture of the Middle Ages is a visual culture, and that the masses learn the teachings of the faith through their eyes. Thus the importance of the *Commentary* and its illustrations cannot be overemphasized. Mâle has shown that it exercised considerable influence during the Romanesque period, despite profound differences in style; concerning its influence in the ninth and tenth centuries we lack positive expressions of appreciation. There is no doubt, however, that these beautiful manuscripts made an impression on many of the faithful, and that they had begun to make their influence felt before the renaissance of sculpture in the grand manner.

Besides, they were not alone. Side by side with the Mozarabic there are Carolingian Apocalypses, and their tradition continues under the Ottonians and even later; the Bamberg Apocalypse, for example, may be considered a belated monument of the style. One or the other served as the model, more or less, for the great apocalyptic scenes painted upon the walls of churches in the eleventh and twelfth centuries. Of the painting in St. Benoît-sur-Loire we possess a description in verse, and time has left untouched a part of the apocalyptic scenes on the ground level and the upper story of the porch of St. Savin-sur-Gartempe of which Yoshikawa, following Elisa Maillard, has recently made a study.[5] We are thus not dealing here with a mere episode; nor is it confined to Spain, southern France, and the Empire, since a manuscript from Cambrai allows us to establish the French and Gothic derivation of an

---

5 I. Yoshikawa, *L'Apocalypse de Saint-Savin*, Paris, 1939.

Anglo-Norman branch. The thought of the Apocalypse accompanies the Middle Ages all along, and not just in the contortions of heresy or in the secrecy of small underground sects, but out in the open; it is offered for the instruction of all men. The fact is proved not only by the tympans showing the Last Judgment, but by the tapestries of the Apocalypse of Angers designed by Jean de Bruges and executed by Nicolas Bataille about 1370. Add, further, that in the moments of a heightened faith—for instance at the time when the Reformation is imminent, from the end of the fifteenth century onward—apocalyptic thought reawakens in a somewhat explosive form: it is the inspiration of Dürer's woodcuts. Apocalyptic thought can be traced much later; we may say that every time mankind is shaken to its depths by a political, military, or moral cataclysm, it will evoke the Apocalypse. Among those who burn with the ardor of a visionary Catholicism, Claudel's genius once more has interpreted and commented, for our frightened age, the Book that foretells and describes the drama of the last days.

If the Apocalypse and the apocalyptic commentaries show such a strong continuity through the centuries, if they accompany mankind's great moments of anxiety, if they sustain the faith of the evangelical reformers from Joachim of Flora to Protestantism, they may be regarded as an essential element of religious thought in the West. But the Apocalypse is not necessarily linked with millenarianism; on the contrary, it necessarily tends to break that link, whether the millennium be that of Augustus or whether it has been adjourned, since the date of the world's end remains ambiguous after the year 1000. Can we doubt that the number one-thousand is understood as symbolic? In any event, in the Church's doctrine God alone has authority to determine the terrible moment, God alone knows the term. Our question is whether the men of the tenth century understood the matter in this way, and whether they, on the eve of the days when Augustine's millennium was about to come to an end, did not feel on their shoulders the weight of its immediate menace.

7. Narthex, Church of Tournus. Late tenth century, early eleventh century. (*Photograph:* Archives Photographiques.)

A diffuse feeling of the "evening of the world" shows itself in the Western Middle Ages well before the fateful date. The expression *mundus senescit* bespeaks not merely the sadness of a disheartened spirit witnessing the progressive decline of civilization, a steady lowering of the human level after the Germanic invasions; nor does it bespeak a purely intellectual pessimism. It surely goes hand in hand with a religious conviction. The world is like a living being which, having passed its maturity, has entered upon old age and, as the Apostle foretold it, must now die. We do not strain the two words of the text by thus giving them the fullness of their meaning. We encounter an analogous and even stronger conviction in the eighth century, in the Life of St. Pardulphus (787). It is expressed categorically, in the formulary of chancery documents composed by the monk Markulf in the seventh century: *Mundi terminum ruinis crescentibus appropinquantem indicia certa manifestant*—"Clear signs announce the end of the world; the ruins multiply." The passage seems to prove that the chronology of the millennium still remains quite uncertain. The very words show a mixture of certainty and vagueness. We meet with them again in the ninth century, in more than one act of donation. It is curious to note that they become rarer in the tenth century. Still, we have examples of them in western and southern France, among others in a donation of Arnulf, Count of Carcassonne and Comminges, to the abbey of Lézat (944): "*Mundi termino appropinquante. . . .*" and in the foundation charter of the priory of Saint-Germain of Muret (948): "*Appropinquante etenim mundi termino et ruinis crescentibus. . . .*" [6] Are these mere turns of phrase taken mechanically from an ancient formulary? Yes, in a sense— but their content, even though used in keeping with a century-old habit, is no less authentic than that of the formula "In the name of the Father, and of the Son, and of the Holy Spirit." In any case, we must remember those dates. The second third of the tenth century presents us with other facts that we must take into ac-

[6] On these charters, see Jules Roy, *L'an mil. Formation de la légende de l'an mil; état de la France de l'an 950 à 1050*, Paris, 1885, pp. 188ff.

count in our examination of the belief in the sunset of the world.
Even earlier, in 909, the Council of Trosly asked the bishops to be
prepared to give an account of their actions, because the Day of
Judgment was coming. But toward the middle of the tenth century an intense movement, a crisis, seems to have arisen.

To this period, in fact, belong two events reported by Abbon of
Fleury, born about 940. In his youth in Paris, he had heard a
preacher announcing the end of the world for the year 1000, to
be followed shortly by the Last Judgment. He also relates a rumor
current in Lorraine: the world will end in the year in which the
Feast of the Annunciation falls on Good Friday. These rumors
were in circulation about 975. But that coincidence of the two
feasts had occurred since the first century, before repeating itself in 992. The *Apologia* of Abbon dates from 998.[7] When the
future abbot of Fleury raised his voice against the Parisian
preacher and the commotion in Lorraine, he applied the wise and
prudent doctrine of the Church, as did all those ecclesiastical authors who came after him: we must not assign a date to the Last
Judgment, we must not force the secret of Providence. His book,
written two years before the year 1000, dealt perhaps with current affairs. Still, between the years 940 and 970, certain charters,
a sermon, a popular rumor give irrefutable testimony of the belief
in the imminence of the world's end. Despite the doubtful character of the chronicle of John the Tritheist (not an original source
properly speaking because it dates from the sixteenth century),
we cannot totally disregard the story of Bernard of Thuringia,
which John places in the year 960. The story is in a way confirmed
by the facts we have recalled and which are more or less contem-
poraneous: the hermit, John reports, appeared before an assembly
of barons to announce the coming of the last day which God had
revealed to him.

We are thus justified in stating that toward the middle and at
the beginning of the second half of the tenth century there ap-

8. Capital, St. Michel Chapel, Tournus. Late tenth, early eleventh century. (*Photograph*: A. Liebreich.)

peared in France, in Lorraine, and in Thuringia a recrudescence of the doctrine of the end of the world and, perhaps, of millenarianism. It found expression not only in the chanceries, but in the Church and in the consciousness of the people. It affected other circles besides, which felt the need to oppose it. In 954 Adso, at the request of Queen Gerberga, wife of Louis IV, composed his book *Libellus de Antechristo*, a book so famous that it has been attributed at times to St. Augustine, at times to Hrabanus Maurus Magnentius.[8] But to make such an attribution is to misunderstand a personality of considerable stature, the energetic reformer of the great abbey of Montiérender in the Champagne, the builder or at least initiator of that lovely church which was consecrated to his successor abbot Berenger at the end of the tenth century. The political interest of the work has not remained a secret to the historians of the Middle Ages, who saw it precisely as a proof of the endurance of the imperial idea in the West after the Carolingian Empire had fallen apart—and not merely of the imperial idea, but of the Frankish imperial idea. Kleinclausz,[9] and after him Fliche,[10] have rightly stressed this aspect of Adso's treatise. But the book is of equal interest to our inquiry. There is no need to fear the end of the world, and the coming of the Antichrist, as long as the kingdoms are not separated from the Roman Empire of which they formed the constituent parts. The time has not come. True, the Empire is in large part destroyed. But as long as the Franks have kings to uphold that Empire, its dignity will not crumble entirely, it will be maintained in their kings. In fact, our doctors have informed us that a king of the Franks, at the end of time, will be the master of the entire Roman Empire, that he will be the greatest and the last of the kings. After a rule of wisdom

8 On Adso, see J. Roy, *op. cit.* pp. 186ff.; the text of the *Libellus* is in Migne, PL, CI, col. 1289ff.; see also E. Amann and E. Dumas, *Histoire de l'Église*, Vol. 7, "L'Église au pouvoir des laïques," Paris, 1948, p. 518.
9 G. Bayet, C. Pfister, and A. Kleinclausz, *"Le christianisme," "Les Barbares," "Merovingiens et Carolingiens,"* in *Historie de France*, by E. Lavisse, Paris, 1903, Vol. II, Part 1, pp. 550ff.
10 A. Fliche, *L'Europe occidentale de 888 à 1125*, Paris, 1940, pp. 132ff.

he will finally go to Jerusalem, to lay his scepter and his crown down on Mount Olivet.

They are impressive pages, which show us the doctrine of the Church united to a political idea. The doctrine of the Church: it is not given to man to set the date of the end of the world, which is the secret of Divine Providence. A political idea: the imperial vocation of the Franks is not spent; although the Empire is destroyed and its kingdoms are separated, there are still Frankish kings who *shall* uphold the Empire—it is their proper privilege and mission. One might imagine that the clever Adso does not let himself forget that he is writing for the spouse of a Carolingian king, and that the very dignity of the recipient inspires him to a reasoning which is likely to reassure her on the destiny of the world, and at the same time on the future of her race. This confidence of a Gaulish abbot in the imperial mission of the Frankish monarchy—coming at the very verge of the time when the Empire will in fact be rebuilt on totally different foundations and to the benefit of the House of Saxony—has a certain pathos.

The parts of the work dealing specifically with the Antichrist are of no smaller interest, because they, too, tend to oppose the belief in the evening of the world. Not only is an end of time impossible so long as the Frankish kings uphold the Empire, but it could not arrive before the great apostasy foretold by St. Paul. Of Antichrist himself, whom he tends to confuse with the Beast of the Apocalypse, Adso gives us the entire history, which is to some extent the counterpart of the life of Christ. Antichrist will be born of the tribe of Dan, in Babylon, and will rebuild the Temple of Jerusalem. His reign will last three and a half years, the forty-two months foretold in the Apocalypse whose chronology—within the millennium, or over and above it—had been studied by St. Augustine. Even though these events are ascribed to a future still beyond view, the Antichrist has had, and always will have, his votaries. We must be careful not to believe that the Antichrist has come every time we witness the appearance of a monster of impiety. This warning helps us to understand certain texts of the second half of the tenth century, in which the disorders of the time are depicted so as to serve a specific cause, and which must not be taken literally, despite their apocalyptic tone. There is, for instance, the famous apostrophe of Arnulf, Bishop of Orléans, addressed to the council of St. Basle-de-Verzy, so important in the history of the Church of Gaul and in the career of the future Sylvester II: [11] "One would say that the Antichrist is ruling us. . . ." One would say—but it is not a fact.

Thus we have established that in the middle of the tenth century there existed a movement, a groundswell of the belief that the world was drawing to a close; and that movement existed also, though more vaguely, in the seventh and eighth centuries. We can even establish its chronology. Between 940 and 950 in southern France, certain charters take up again the sorrowful expressions of the formulary of Markulf which had fallen somewhat into disuse during the preceding century, doubtless in response to the Empire's restoration by the Carolingians. The coming of the Antichrist was expected next in 954, since Adso then wrote his *Libellus* to refute that idea. In 958, Abbon was a novice at Fleury; when he was a youth, that is, close to that year, he heard the sermon, in Paris, about the approaching end of the world. In 960, Bernard, the hermit of the Thuringian province, announces that God has revealed to him the imminent end of the world. Ten or fifteen years later the idea spreads again, and we meet it once more in Abbon's *Apologia:* "I have opposed with all my strength this opinion [of the coming of the Antichrist at the turn of a thousand years], with the gospels, the Apocalypse, and the Book of Daniel; Abbot Richard of blessed memory, having received from Lorraine letters on the subject, ordered me to reply." [12] Everything leads us to think that the movement swells like a tide as the century moves toward its end, and the year 1000 is the culmination of these terrors.

---

[11] A. Olleris, *Œuvres de Gerbert*, Paris and Clermont, 1867, p. 213.
[12] Abbon, Letter X (Migne, PL, CXXXIX, col. 471).

II

It is remarkable that we find no trace of it in the official documents or in the chroniclers of the times. The fact is all the more extraordinary because, once the terminal year of the millennium has passed, the belief in the end of the world spreads with renewed vigor in the course of the eleventh century. Neither in the protocol nor in the official speeches of Robert the Pious, King of France in the year 1000, do we find any of the old formulas on the sunset of the world; Pfister [13] reports nothing but "banal reflections on the need to aid the churches, the abbeys, the servants of God, and to assist the poor and the weak. The King expresses the hope that in return for his good deeds God will protect his kingdom and later grant to him and to his kin life eternal." The same silence prevails in the more than one hundred and fifty papal bulls promulgated between 970 and the year 1000. The same silence again reigns among the annalists of the time, some of whom do not even mention the fateful date—for example Aimoin of Fleury, Odoran of Sens, and Adhémar of Chabannes. It is the same with the biographies of Abbon and of St. Majolus, written in 1000 and 1040, respectively. Glaber, finally, who does believe that the end of time and the reign of Satan are at hand, and who paints the year 1000 in the same somber colors he employs for his whole era, reports no movements corresponding to those we have shown to exist in the middle of the century or, more exactly, in the period from 940 to 970. Better still, Thietmar of Merseburg sees the year 1000 as the very opposite of a year of horror; he interprets it as the comforting thousandth anniversary of the birth of Christ: "When the thousandth year since the salvific birth of the Immaculate Virgin had come, a radiant dawn rose over the world." [14] I refuse to see in this text the pure and simple statement that it was a fine day. We have a right to ask ourselves whether we must not on the

[13] C. Pfister, *Etudes sur le règne de Robert le Pieux* (996–1031), Paris, 1885, p. xxvii.

[14] Thietmar of Merseburg, *Chronique* (Mon. Germ. Hist., Script. III), 790.

contrary see in it an intentional reaction against widespread fears, one more example of the Church's attitude toward millenarianism, and perhaps also the expression of political optimism among the chroniclers of the Saxon emperors.

It might be thought that the belief in the world's end is dead and mankind reassured. The fatal day is past, the world goes on, we may be at peace. But the old fear has lost nothing of its power; although we possess no indication that there was terror at the critical moment, we do have positive information concerning the fear of the world's end which sprung up very soon after. In the documents mentioned by Jules Roy,[15] concerning the same region as the charters of 944 and 948—a restitution made to the Abbey of Lézat in 1030, and a quittance for the same abbey in 1048—we meet again the phrase from Markulf's formulary: *Appropinquante etenim mundi termino et ruinis crescentibus*; perhaps it is repeated, after all, as a stereotyped convention in a remote chancery, but it undeniably corresponds also to a certain state of belief. In this respect, Jerusalem seems to have been what might be called a crystallizing point. In writing of a journey which Odolric, bishop of Orléans, made in 1028 to the Holy Land, Glaber tells us that the unheard-of eagerness of the people in Jerusalem was the sign which, according to the pilgrims themselves, announced the infamous Antichrist whose coming is in fact expected just before the end of time.[16] According to William Godel,[17] a monk from the Limousin who tells of the events of the years 1009–1010, many people believed that the end of the world was coming when Jerusalem was taken. During the last years of the eleventh century—the days when Emperor Henry IV ruled in the West and Emperor Alexius in Byzantium—the Saxon annalist reports that calamities were multiplying everywhere—wars, famines, and plagues—as well as baneful portents, and throughout all the nations the heavenly trumpet heralded the coming of the Supreme Judge.

15 J. Roy, *op. cit.*, p. 188.
16 R. Glaber, *Histoires*, Book IV, Ch. 6; E. Pognon, *op. cit.*, p. 123.
17 Cited in J. Roy, *op. cit.*, p. 180.

We are faced with a paradoxical situation: for the middle of the tenth century and all through the eleventh, we possess either compelling proof, or else significant traces, of the belief in the world's end; for the years immediately before the year 1000 and for that year itself, we no longer have any. The decisive moment, it would seem, left men indifferent. Must we agree with Pfister that what I have called the crisis of the tenth century (a somewhat strong and dramatic term) was no more than a small, obscure heresy successfully opposed by the Church? Must we believe that the obsession with the end of the world, or rather the fear of the Last Judgment, had in the end become separated from Augustines' calculation of the millennium, so that men could, and even had to, go on reading John's Apocalypse and dreading the terrible consummation, but without embracing millenarian doctrines? I do not think that the fear of the tenth century can be interpreted as a heresy in the strict sense. The Church could treat it in that fashion; but it reflects a state of mind that is almost permanent in certain circles, in the Middle Ages, while other circles at the same period thought, felt, and acted differently. History includes both rational and irrational elements. Among the former belong the phenomena of structure, the great political and economic combinations, and certain well-defined movements of thought. The latter allow us to enter into areas of human life much less clearly defined, much less easily understood, because the affective values live in the eternal twilight of the instincts. It may be said that there are two races of men at work, at the same time and in the same places, but working wholly different lines. The closing years of the tenth century, including the year 1000 itself, and the opening years of the eleventh show the most energetic builders of the West at work, sound and clear minds filled with ideas that are both large and concrete even when they harbor certain impossible dreams—great princes, great prelates, heads of religious orders, women of action, superb observers of history who see and speak clearly, such as Richerus, pupil of Gerbert. There is, in short, an entire, well-fashioned superstructure of human beings. Below it there are shadowy zones, enormous strength and weakness, waves of faith, courage, despair, and fear. As we shall see, the year 1000 presents a picture of strong contrasts. While there is no text that allows us to assert that in its obscure strata it was shaken by the fear of the world's end, yet fear—an ill-defined fear feeding on everything—was dominant nonetheless. That fear exceeds the year in point of time, it was present earlier and does not end when the year ends. True, it did not defeat Western man; he goes about his business under a sky heavy with portent. But there is surely no more truth to the "radiant dawn" of Thietmar of Merseburg than there is to the night of terror of the romantic historians.

Let us take Glaber, who remains our best source for this strange period and whose interest is far from exhausted. He is valuable for his factual documentation, but valuable also as a personal and, to revive a worn-out expression, human document. No one can doubt that his information was considerable. He had been taught at Cluny, where everything was known. He has, however, no principle of order, no critical sense; he does possess—and this is in the eyes of modern historians a more serious failing—the artist's gifts, those of a visionary artist. He is a sort of crude apocalyptic genius, who paints not only facts and men but also their nimbus of prodigies. At moments there occurs in his faded Latin—which is so different from the beautiful Ciceronian elegance of the Gerbertains—some highly felicitous expression which brings an image of life and rewards the reader. It is interesting to observe how Pfister, so admirably neat in his studies of the reign of Robert the Pious—where everything is in place and always in the right light (save, perhaps, the humanity of those days)—battles with that imprecision which is natural to our author, and how he allows his irritation to pierce the impersonal severity of his language.[18] Gebhart moves on a different ground, one he knows well, and for which he shows a taste and a fine sensitivity, as he attempts to understand the human being of the year 1000 through the monk of the year 1000; he does not totally neglect the other aspect, the other

[18] C. Pfister, op. cit., pp. 110–114.

exemplars of man, though to my mind he does not allow them enough play.

Glaber's biography has been established by the learned Burgundian scholar Ernest Petit,[19] especially the beginning of his monastic career, which starts early: at the age of twelve he wears the habit. Indeed, Glaber's life was spent in various regions of Burgundy, first at St. Germain in Auxerre under Abbot Helderic, between 997 and 1004 or 1005, with a brief stay at St. Léger of Champeaux. After leaving Auxerre he lives for five or six years at Moûtiers-St. Jean. From 1015 to 1035 he is a monk at St. Bénigne in Dijon, under Abbot William, though for short intervals he stays in other abbeys, at Bèze and at Suze. From 1030 to 1035 we find him at Cluny, under St. Odilo. He finally returns to the abbey of his young days, St. Germain of Auxerre, which he leaves only briefly for Moûtiers-en-Puisaye and where he ends his days. In the course of his travels from abbey to abbey he has known at least two great personages, William of Volpiano, abbot of St. Bénigne, and St. Odilo, abbot of Cluny. He spent his life in a region where major events—the conquest of Burgundy by Robert the Pious— were taking place. Finally, he was a guest in more than one house of distinction, and had also had the advantage of traveling the great roads and seeing the world. He is not altogether a man of the cloistered cell who labors in the silence of a solitary life; he had journeyed here and there, had met the living, breathing beings of this world, he had known the year 1000, not through texts but by living it and feeling its wind in his face. Besides, he had gone beyond the frontiers of the province; in 1028, Abbot William had taken him along to Italy. There is something nomadic about his life.

The truth is that his turbulence caused him to be thrown out of more than one monastery. It seems that from his youth up he was possessed by that demon of good and bad jokes, and by that instinct for dissent of which his compatriots are not always inno-

[19] E. Petit, "Raoul Glaber," *Revue Historique*, 1892.

cent. He admits his faults with a candor that wins our sympathy. We are not dealing here with a mystic consumed by the ardors of the cloister, but with a fine fellow who had been packed off to the convent by an uncle when he had barely ceased being a child. In another age, Raoul Glaber would have become one of those country priests who are so typically French, warm-hearted, glad of the good things of life, splendid ministers, well-read in the old style. Well-read he certainly was, and when he was given the door by this or that monastery, he took it philosophically, in the full conviction that his knowledge would always open some other abbey door to him. He was called on to perform certain modest tasks, such as the restoration of the epitaphs at St. Germain of Auxerre that were worn with age. An unruly character? Certainly—but this brisk Burgundian is a far cry from the bandit monks of Farfa who, after an initial revolt in 936, proceeded to poison their abbot Dagobert, and prolonged their bacchanalia until the reign of Otto III (983). He is equally remote from those wandering monks of the eleventh century who went about celebrating the mass of the divine Bacchus in the most elegant Latin. Glaber's Latin—he wrote some short obituary notes, some chapters in his chronicles —bears no resemblance at all to that diabolical paganism, first tremor of the Renaissance to shake the obscure clergy. He is too timid to be clearly a bad monk, a *rerum novarum studiosus*.

He is afraid of the imminent end of the world. To him, the year 1000 is not a date like any other: "Satan will soon be unleashed because the thousand years have been completed." The Demon prowls and stalks man from eternity, but more than ever during these troubled years. Glaber has seen him more than once, at one time even standing next to his pillow. The Demon is a small black monster of human shape. Sick people must be wary of his tricks and distrust him constantly. The prince of metamorphoses has the gifts of ubiquity and multiplicity. His favorite haunts are trees and springs. How can we fail to hear in these warnings the echo of those ancient Celtic beliefs concerning not just trees and springs, but also rocks and megalithic monuments—beliefs against which numerous councils of the High Middle Ages have raised their voice, as did an edict of Charlemagne, late in the eighth century? In its deepest human substrata, the year 1000 thus preserved deposits of prehistory, which the clerics interpreted in a rather Manichean manner, ill-defined but present all the same.

He is fearful of Satan, "who will soon appear because the thousand years have been completed," but he is fearful also of the God of wrath, Satan's old adversary, who is multiplying the portents and signs of damnation. And now a frightening meteor crosses the sky of the year 1000:

It appeared in the month of September, not long after nightfall, and remained visible for nearly three months. It shone so brightly that its light seemed to fill the greater part of the sky, then it vanished at cock's crow. But whether it is a new star which God launches into space, or whether He merely increases the normal brightness of another star, only He can decide who in the mysterious secrecy of His wisdom prepares all things. What appears established with the greatest degree of certainty is that this phenomenon in the sky never appears to men without being the sure sign of some mysterious and terrible event. And indeed a fire soon consumed the church of St. Michael the Archangel, built on a promontory in the ocean, which had always been the object of special veneration throughout the whole world.[20]

This comet or some prodigy of the same order is doubtless the occasion for the *Miracles de saint Aile*, depicting for us fiery armies fighting in the sky. In order to ward off this portent, the abbess of Jouarre, Ermengarde, and Renard, the abbot of Rebais, started a procession. These young nuns and religious people filing past in prayer, lead by their spiritual heads, under the conflagration in the sky—what a picture they make of anguished humanity! But they do not allow us to conclude that the millenarian terrors were authentic, because the text does not mention the end of the world. We add this text to the archives of fear, so richly stocked

[20] R. Glaber, *Histories*, Book III, Ch. 3; E. Pognon, *op. cit.*, pp. 87–88; and see J. Roy, *op. cit.*, pp. 204–205.

for the period that concerns us. But it would be unsound, even false reasoning to assert that the comet of the year 1000 is not the sole example of a prodigy in the sky during the period, and to cite the letter of King Robert to his half-brother Goslin, abbot of St. Benoît-sur Loire, concerning another meteor that appeared in 1022.[21] Apart from the fact that mankind is forever in the habit of trembling before unusual phenomena, even if they occur repeatedly, future events did not affect the men of the year 1000, simply because they obviously did not know what would happen twenty years later. What moves men to their depths is the frightful evidence of what goes on before their eyes. Otherwise, the event of 1022 clearly shows how the effects on men's minds differ according to their condition. The masses are afraid. They turn to prayer. Abbot Goslin returns to the *Book of Wonders* of Valerius Rufus and the *Ecclesiastical History* of Eusebius; his explanation seems entirely candid to us, but even so it is an attempt at interpretation.

Such was the psychology of fear, an astounding thing in Glaber's contemporaries, and all the more astounding in Glaber himself because he was not an *illuminatus* but a hard-headed, stubborn Burgundian. Let us refrain, then, from enlarging on the matter by describing the calamities that beset the end of the tenth century, epidemics such as that of St. Anthony's fire raging with mortal fury in 977; Lieutard's heresy, which may well be a sporadic and even spontaneous outburst related to Catharist doctrine; and finally the great famines that had assumed what must be called an endemic character in those grim days. But the manner in which Glaber reports the most terrible of these famines is thought-provoking. He tells us: "Men believed that the orderly procession of the seasons and the laws of nature, which until then had ruled the world, had relapsed into the eternal chaos; and they feared that mankind would end." He is speaking of the great famine of 1033.[22] Glaber informs us that it occurred in *the year 1000 after*

21 *Receuil des historiens des Gaules et de la France*, Vol. X.
22 R. Glaber, *Histoires*, Book IV, Ch. 4; E. Pognon, *op. cit.*, pp. 116–120.

the Passion. To my mind, this is certainly a touch of what I would call belated millenarianism. The world had not come to an end in the year 1000 after the Incarnation. But there is a year 1000 after the Passion, and "men feared that mankind would end." Thus fear swings from one date to another, according to how the millennium is computed. We catch that fear at work in a text that cannot be disputed. While it is true that the fear of seeing all mankind die of hunger is not the same as dreading the end of the world, it is not far from it, especially if we consider the formulation of the report. I add that we have other expressions of Glaber's personal millenarianism, which seems to me established beyond cavil. He uses the year 1000 as a sort of pivot or landmark by which to place facts in the course of time. The earth is putting on the pure white robe of churches in "the third year after the year 1000." Besides, man never was more evil and more corrupt, vice never more rampant with a more apocalyptic fury. We have not heard the last word.[23]

Let us rehearse once more the elements of our question. In 954, Adso addressed to Queen Gerberga a treatise designed to oppose the belief in the imminent appearance of the Antichrist, which is the prelude to the end of the world. In 960, Bernard the hermit announces the end of the world as it has been revealed to him. In 970, the rumor spreads through Lorraine that the end of the world is near. In 1009, in Jerusalem, men believe that the end of the world has come. In 1033, in Gaul, men believe that mankind will perish. In the year 1000 a prodigy in the sky, which men interpret as a sign of God's wrath, portends frightful calamities. The chronicler of the year 1000, Glaber, lives in terror, the reign of Satan is at hand. To him, the year 1000 is not the year 999 plus one. It, or rather the number 1000, has a mysterious meaning, whether the count begins with the Incarnation of Christ or with his Passion. Yet not one text on that date makes mention of collective terrors

[23] Dom François Plaine, "Les prétendues terreurs de l'an mil," *Revue des questions historiques,* 1873.

or waves of fear. When the critical moment comes, when the fatal term is reached, the men who earlier were fearful of the end of time and who would afterward exhibit the same dread, felt reassured and confident. There is something strange here.

Are we to believe that the years immediately before the year 1000 were such as to dispel all fears? What matters is not our own feelings, our interpretation as objective historians, but the state of mind of the contemporaries. We return to the address of Arnulf, bishop of Orléans, to the Council of St. Basle-de-Verzy. I feel justified in doing so, since I have shown that the concluding allusion to the Antichrist had no positive value, but was a natural "movement" or "effect" in a diatribe against the papacy. But the summaries of the misfortunes of Christianity retain their full value:

O days of misery! In what town shall we find support now that Rome, the Queen of Nations, has been despoiled of her human and divine powers? Let us admit resolutely, let us say it out loud, that Rome, after the fall of the Empire, has lost the Church of Alexandria, she has lost the Church of Antioch; and today we witness that Europe —not to speak of Africa and Asia—wishes to separate itself from Rome. The Church of Constantinople has withdrawn from her jurisdiction, central Spain will not accept her judgments, *we all are witnesses of the revolt of which the Apostle speaks*—a revolt not just of people but of Churches. The agents of the Pope who come to Gaul oppress us with all their might. One would say that the Antichrist is ruling us.[24]

There is no need to question whether the final phrase is purely allegorical or has a political thrust. Nor shall I make much of this other phrase: "We all are witnesses of the revolt of which the Apostle speaks." But it is obvious that Christianity, and in particular the Church, was in a woeful state at the end of the tenth century, and that the most enlightened minds were sadly aware of

[24] This text by Arnulf is contained in Gerbert's report of the Council: A. Olleris, *op. cit.*, p. 213.

it: Arnulf does not hesitate to allude to the time foretold in the Apocalypse. France herself was beset by the greatest misfortunes of all. Perhaps this is not correct historically, but morally it is a fact. In France, Glaber informs us, the Church of Christ is stricken with the most fearful calamities, of which certain elemental signs had given warning, but the king, aided by Divine protection, stayed their course. These "certain signs" multiply in the year 1000: besides the comet of which Raoul Glaber speaks, we must mention the apparition of a dragon in the sky and an earthquake, reported by Sigebert of Gembloux and in the chronicle of Saint-Médard of Soissons. The state of Christianity, the state of France, the large number of dire portents—everything comes together, everything converges and points to terror. The year 1000, then, was not a year of respite between crises.

We must look elsewhere, then, for the explanation of this apparent peace in the souls of men, and this—relative—silence in the contemporary texts. That explanation can be found only in the prudent policy of the Church, a policy which had found its expression in Adso's *Libellus* and in the assignment with which the abbot Richard had entrusted Abbon. What is at work here— besides humaneness of a high degree—is a signal canonical prudence, for the Church had no interest in seeing facts giving the lie to a revealed text. To the superior minds, and even to minds that were merely enlightened, the validity of the Apocalypse remained wholly incontestable, but that validity was in some way timeless, a kind of perpetual calendar of the deep anxieties of the human soul, of this fear of the judgment without which Christian faith loses an aspect of tremendous poetic power, as well as a very efficacious threat. That doctrine of an adjournment *sine die* which arose in the second third of the tenth century would thus have borne fruit.

Yet the unusual facets in the state of men's souls remain all the same, and the heresy of Lieutard, which we have mentioned, is merely one of many. This type of religious despair, together with the refusal to pay the tithe, this crucifix trampled underfoot, is the mark of a man so overcome by suffering that he no longer hopes for anything. Can it be also that some vague millenarian feeling prompted the first stirring of that evangelic purism, the Catharist doctrine? The obsession with the "nightfall of the world," the "great nightfall," exercises all religious reformers—including those mighty organizers of a civilization in the Western desert of the United States, the "Latter Day Saints."

In our attempt to define and classify these evanescent data, it may behoove us to recall, as suggested in our introduction, that a period or a society is not entirely of a piece, but consists of several levels of humanity—in short, to propose a kind of moral geology. On the oldest level we find the man of prehistory, always present and hidden, bluntly exposed at moments by the convulsion of time—time, the butcher of human flesh who digs up corpses at night in the graveyards to sell them in his shop. To a more peaceful and more mysterious region, but also stemming from the dim past, belong the faithful of ancient secular cults that know no death and that have been preserved down to our day in folklore—the religion of trees, springs, and rocks. Above these are the middle strata of Christianity, abounding with emotional appeal and powerful mass instincts; the faithful frightened by portents, shaken by sermons, carried away by waves of collective beliefs; the crowds that are deeply stirred by the revelation of the secrets hidden in the scriptures, and are always ready to be amazed by numerology, with its false air of certainty. Their idea of nature is still animistic and dramatic, closer to the ancient Jewish Bible than to the gospels. Mingling with these crowds are sporadic nonbelievers full of fury—surely more numerous than we think, even in the upper classes—such as Aimoin, Count of Sens, who was called the King of the Jews because he loved them, although he piled the grossest insults upon priests and even prelates. Finally, there are the organic forces, those that are sustaining and constructive. They are only slightly affected by the errors of the masses; from our period onward, there are among them not only what we call enlightened minds, but men of high and radiant intelligence. They have a true understanding of the absolute—that is, metaphysical —value of certain articles of faith, but also of their merely relative value in the conduct of human affairs. History is perhaps only a series of interchanges and mutual adjustments among these various stratifications, exhibiting sudden breaches that lay bare the secrets of the depths. This is how I see the year 1000. We cannot state with absolute certainty that the year was shaken by those collective terrors which we note thirty years earlier and cannot find again afterward, but their absence remains a surprise to us. In any event, it is certain that the effort to organize the West, which was made during this period, grew out of altogether different human soil from that which could have nourished this tormented psychology.

TWO

The Building of the West

AT the end of the tenth century and the beginning of the eleventh, the West as I have defined it—the peoples fronting on the Atlantic, among whom Spain and France also touch the Mediterranean—presents a variety of aspects, some of which belong to the Carolingian world while others herald and prepare the Romanesque world. Every period in history, indeed every moment in history, is a product of the encounter between past and future, and the proportion of their mixture may well define what we call the present. The "present" of the year 1000 exhibits forms of great antiquity side by side with forms destined to great future growth, constructive phenomena that renew historic life and phenomena of dissolution that cause the past to disappear. In using these terms—"constructive phenomena," "the building of the West"—I do not, however, imply a systematic will or an overall plan. Man may influence events and alter their course by maintaining a harmony with them that is extremely subtle and finely shaded. The works of pure spirit, driven by force into the moving substance of time, rarely endure, because they do not take sufficient account of life. The year 1000 offers a remarkable example, in the attempt at universal monarchy made by Otto III and Gerbert.

A fact decisive for the future of the world, and in particular for the fate of the Romanesque world, is the retreat of Islam and the decline of the caliphate of Cordova at the end of the tenth century. Besieged by the infidels and invaded by the barbarians, Christianity begins at this point to regain the upper hand, both in the East, where the Bagratid princes proceed to reconquer Armenia, and in the regions of central Europe, where the Hungarians (who at the height of the tenth century had burned the monasteries of Gaul) have, at the founding of the apostolic monarchy in the year 1000, faced about to oppose the people of the steppes, and become the defenders of Christian Europe. The retreat, the turnabout, and the halt of the barbarians—lured on by Charles the Simple, who had ceded certain maritime regions of the lower Seine to a Norman pirate chief—inaugurate the Middle Ages in the strict sense, just as the Germanic invasions inaugurate the High Middle Ages. We cannot lay too much stress on these exactly inverse phenomena. Up north, no doubt, the people of the sea are at the height of the great Viking expansion, but by their conversion they have joined or are now joining the Christian community. The young blades of Normandy, horse thieves all, are going to set up a kingdom in southern Italy and Sicily; Duke William is about to conquer England as did Canute the Viking; and until the middle of the fourteenth century, the pirates of Gotland come to sap the Hanseatic towns. But the great political foundations of the Normans, set up on the same sites as the West itself—the most important of them has lasted to this day and brought about the elimination or subjection of the continental Germans settled in England—are no longer a kind of raid and pillage; the Normans now tend to take possession, create stability, set up an order. In the same way, two new powers achieve a stable structure among the ruins of the Carolingian Empire at the end of the tenth century: the Holy Roman Empire of the German Nation, which will endure until 1804, and the Capetian monarchy that is to last until the French Revolution.

Thus we can safely state that the chronological area of the year 1000, and the year 1000 itself, is a great moment in the history of mankind. Before we study its principal episodes, we must look briefly at the conditions of life and the general setting in which the action of history takes its course.

I

The historic landscape of the year 1000 is still wooded as it was in the tenth century; the great European forest covers a large part of the continent, two thirds of Gaul and England, Ireland, the Low Countries, and central Germany. We are less sure of it for northeastern Spain; Puig i Cadafalch believes that the early appearance of vaults of stone construction in Catalonia is due, at least in part, to the abundance of stones and the scarcity of wood, while in the "carpentry bone," which was immense in the tenth century, many churches are covered with wood for precisely the opposite reason. This view may be disputed, but cannot be discarded altogether. We are certain that northern Italy—whose teams of stone masons, famed for their skill, went abroad in search of work—presents the same aspect, and we know from other sources that this region, too, was forest land. The same is true of Scandinavia, especially Norway, where the construction of churches built entirely of wood survives the incursion of the Romanesque style; and it is true of eastern and southeastern Europe—for instance, Poland, Galicia, and the central part of Transylvania, the Bihor massif—where wood is the material of country churches even in the Baroque period.

In this respect, the era of the dissolution of Charlemagne's Empire recalls Merovingian times. Perhaps in this Europe of forests there existed a "wood civilization" analogous to the one of which we find not only traces but living examples in the remote regions of the Carpathian mountains. Strzygowski, taking up again certain ideas of Courajod, has claimed that what I have called "wood civilization" was indeed the starting point of the great medieval cultures. This is an error; it is precisely the return to stone, to lasting materials, that, as we shall soon see, began in the second half of the tenth century to define the outlines of a new expression of life, a new art of understanding form, man, and the world. A little later, it is accompanied by the struggle against the forest and by the clearing and drainage of land, which are among the great tasks of the eleventh century. This is the conquest of the earth for grainland, which was so vigorous in the twelfth century.

The status of landed property is in most cases still defined in terms of the large Carolingian manor. This close manorial fold is among the basic characteristics of the High Middle Ages. Its consequence is the disappearance—not total, but almost so—of all exchange economy. Man lives on the manor, on its resources; manorial industry, with its crude technology, serves to satisfy the needs of a life without luxuries. The descriptions of the large monastic communities which we find in the Carolingian texts, and which are borne out by such documents as the plan for the establishment of St. Gall, with shops and offices where worker-monks are to labor, afford striking examples of a type of life that extended at least until the year 1000 and is by no means limited to the monasteries. What is remarkable, however, is that the small landholding survived along the shores of the Atlantic and the Mediterranean, in ancient Neustria, in Aquitaine, and in Provence, though we can offer no explanation for this fact by recourse to the history of earlier civilizations. We can only note the fact that in the central part, the north, and the northeast of Gaul, large domains under seignorial rule are most frequent, while landholdings remain divided along the edge of the sea. This fact, however, in no way alters the condition of the peasant. There are no more freeholders, or hardly any. The seignorial rights that oppress the man of the soil are crushing. France, in the middle of the tenth century, seems as though it had been taken by conquest only the day before; and what we have is indeed a conquest—of soil and property and even man himself—by the former high Imperial functionaries, who had become hereditary owners of offices and benefices, without the restraining hand of a regulatory power. This is the chaos of the Germanic Middle Ages, while an Empire is disintegrating; it shows the frightful consequences of a rapacity which, to satisfy its greed for immediate profit, drains the source of its own wealth by the proliferation, for example, of road and market tolls that empty the roads, bridges, and ports of traffic. Richerus and Flodoard, in turn, inform us of the ravages of the countryside through invasions and wars, and Raoul Glaber tells us of famines: forty-eight years of dearth between 970 and 1040; the most terrible among them, the year 1000 and the year 1033, according to our chronicler, threatened the death of the human race. On men so weakened, epidemics descend like a fire from heaven—*ignis sacer*. It is amazing that social upheavals were not more frequent and more violent under such conditions. I have spoken of the heretic Lieutard, who refused to pay the tithe, and trampled the crucifix underfoot. But it does not appear that any sort of religious feeling played a part, one year earlier, in 997, in the peasant revolt in Normandy.

This is one view of the picture. What makes it gloomy is not the imagination of a raving millenarian, or a romantic historian. For example, Richerus, who witnessed the closing years of the tenth century in Gaul, is a man of sound and solid mind, not some bedazzled peasant given to credulity. A man of good breeding, son of a councillor to Louis IV, and above all a pupil of Gerbert, Richerus is our best source for the history of the revolution of 987, that revolution which replaced the Carolingian dynasty and substituted the Capetians, in the person of Hugh. There is no reason to doubt what he tells us, not so much about the entire human condition as about the state of the countryside until 998, the date with which his *Historia* stops. In a different key, and much less colorfully, he confirms to a large extent what Glaber tells us on the same subject.[1]

But it is certain, on the other hand, that the world's misery in this period is neither continuous nor universal. Pfister rejects the notion that France under Robert the Pious was crushed by misfortunes, and has severe criticism for Glaber's lack of method, his

1 Richerus, *Historiarum libri IV*, ed. Pertz, in *Monumenta Germaniae*, 1833.

credulity, and his uncritical acceptance of each and every rumor.[2] He accuses him especially of misapportioning his descriptions of the great famines, that of 1002–1003 and, a few pages further on, that of 1033. All this, in the view of the learned historian, lacks precision. But the facts remain as they are all the same. Besides, we surely must also take account of the relative prosperity of the towns. Glaber, though he may be untrustworthy concerning the countryside, becomes once more a source worthy of confidence when he gives praise to certain cities: "Orléans is famed for her beauty, the wealth of her citizens, the fertility of her lands, the beauty of her river which makes irrigation an easy matter." To my understanding, these texts are not contradictory. It is possible, alas, to starve in a city that is well constructed, well situated, rich and populous, and surrounded by fertile lands. Bernard of Hersfeld, it is true, praises the prosperity of France during this period: "Among all the lands Gaul is the most fertile in the abundance of her yield; moreover, she is devoted to the liberal arts and strictly observes monastic discipline."[3] It is not much, but it is enough to make us understand that this country, though beset by undeniably severe plagues, had more abundant resources than other countries; this allowed her to resist.

It is, besides, quite certain that from this period on—the reign of Robert—the urban character of the Capetian monarchy becomes more clearly defined. It can hardly be disputed that her princes were country squires, hunters, and warriors, and thus continued a secular tradition, but part of their support came from the fine towns. These towns were not built yesterday. They constitute, no doubt, the point of strongest contrast between the West, especially Gaul, and central Europe, save for the Rhine, whose banks were studded with Roman colonies. In Germany, Charlemagne and his successors had to start from nothing. In Gaul the towns, though sinking into poverty and obsolescence under the Mero-

[2] C. Pfister, *Études sur le règne de Robert le Pieux*, Paris, 1885, pp. 110ff.
[3] Text in Mabillon, *Acta Sanctorum Ordinis Sancti Benedicti*, saec. IV, vol. II, p. 364.

vingians and Carolingians, remained standing on their ancient foundations; they were extremely numerous, not only in the Dominion in the strict sense, but in the great feudal estates: in the south and southwest, Arles, Marseilles, Toulouse, Bordeaux, Saintes, and Poitiers; in the north, Boulogne, Noyon, Soissons, Laon, and the acropolis of the last Carolingians, Reims; in the central region, the great Norman towns and the towns of the Seine; in Burgundy, Langres on its mountain top, a town since the most remote times, Auxerre, Dijon still surrounded by the walls of the *castrum*, Autun the Roman town; and everywhere, many other centers that will play a part in reviving the network of French activity. Their role is threefold—they are arsenals, military strongholds, and places of refuge; they are also religious centers if they are bishoprics or, like Dijon, the seat of a great abbey; finally, they are markets. In a period when the economy of exchange is still so weak, the extent of urban business transactions is limited, of course. Their activity was no doubt like that of our small towns and boroughs of today, with farmers' markets for a tiny region, and which are so typical a facet of French life. But though the manorial system has long impeded their development, they remained nonetheless centers whose population was dense even if small; they remained clusters of people. This is an essential fact of civilization: whenever men are scattered and separated from their fellows by empty gaps, or only from small groups, wherever they are little stimulated by new contracts, there civilization recedes.

It is regrettable that we do not have for the towns of the year 1000 anything comparable to Ferdinand Lot's splendid studies of the Merovingian towns, or Pirenne's work on the towns from the eleventh century onward. We are in danger of either overstating or understating the importance of the texts, according to our inclination. But archaeology serves us well, because it shows us the number and the purpose of the royal foundations in our towns. There is something impressive even in the driest catalogue of these foundations which we owe to Robert the Pious, and from which we offer here just a few examples: in Orléans, his home town and his favorite, *regia urbs, regum Francorum principalis sedes regia,* he erected St. Aignan, two churches dedicated to Our Lady, and not far from them the great state prison where Charles, duke of Lower Lorraine, was confined; in Paris, whose county was the basis of the historic fortune of Robert and his heirs, he raised an impressive palace, *palatium insigne,* with a chapel dedicated to St. Nicholas, and the two churches of St. Germain-des-Prés and St. Germain-l'Auxerrois; at Étampes, another palace and the abbey of Notre-Dame; at Melun, the abbey of Notre-Dame and another church; at Senlis, the monasteries of St. Pierre and St. Rieul; at Autun, St. Cassien.[4] The list could be extended, but these examples are enough to prove not only that the towns mattered but that they were chosen for highly important civil and religious foundations which presuppose the presence of a population and a center of activity.[5]

It is true, of course, that these foundations themselves, distributed as they are throughout the entire reign, do not throw light on our question whether the year 1000 and its immediate chronological antecedents represent one of those focuses, one of those high points to which we have alluded. We shall return to the matter when we come to study the history of architecture at this precise moment of its development. With regard to the "renaissance" of the towns and to the economic revival, let us follow Pirenne—we could not have a better guide in these matters: "The famous legend of the terrors of the year 1000 is not without symbolic significance. It is doubtless untrue that the people were expecting the end of the world in the year 1000, but the century opening on that data is characterized, in contrast with the century preceding it, by a rebirth of activity so striking that it could be taken for the awakening of a society which had long been suffering

---

[4] On the foundations of Robert the Pious, see Helgaud, "Vie du roi Robert," *Receuil des Historiens des Gaules et de la France,* Vol. X, col. 115; E. Pognon, *op. cit.,* p. 364.

[5] H. Pirenne, *Les villes du moyen âge,* Brussels, 1927, p. 72.

a painful nightmare." This sentence could serve as a model for all historians who are inclined to jump to conclusions. Yet some remarks are in order. It is not untrue, as we have seen, that certain groups were expecting the end of the world in the year 1000, but it is correct that the Church counteracted the terrors, and that the enlightened classes were probably untouched by them. Yet everything happens exactly as if there had been "suffering" of something "painful," and then an "awakening." Hence the sharp difference between the time which preceded the year 1000 and that which followed it. But it would be poor practice for a historian not to take account of those forces which before that date, toward the end of the tenth century, contribute to the building of the West, and of which the life of the Church presents us with some interesting examples.

II

Arnulf's speech to the Council of St. Basle-de-Verzy has shown us how divided Christendom appeared to his contemporaries, and we must add at once that that impression was correct. The Greek Church stood apart, with its own distinct orthodoxy and political role; what is more, Rome, weakened by the protracted scandals of the popes of Tusculum, was being challenged and opposed in still other quarters than those of Mozarabic Spain. Between the ancient Celtic Christians of Ireland and the "Roman" Church of England, there were not merely disagreements on matters of dogma and liturgy, but a deep and sullen opposition rooted in the customs, turn of mind, and traditions of the opposing groups. Regarding France, the debates of St. Basle-de-Verzy convey an idea of a long-growing bitterness against the Papacy. What we know of the Catharist heresy belongs to a later date, especially to those days when for the first time in our history the secular arm is needed to deal with the canons of Sainte-Croix at Orléans; but it can hardly be doubted that the heresy was fermenting before the year 1000. Finally, there was profound dissension among the clerics themselves, united as they doubtless were in matters of faith—dissension between the regular and secular priesthood and between monks and bishops. Because both groups are feudal lords, their interests may clash; we see armed battle between the bishop's men and the men of the abbot intent on escaping the jurisdiction of the ordinary. Even more, the two are separated by their totally different views on the duties of the Christian life.

The monastic reform of the tenth century, of which Cluny was the driving force, is obviously an important enterprise and rightly stressed by historians, but it is only one episode, though more far-reaching than the others, in a long list of rather extended and violent crises in the life of the medieval monasteries. One might say that in this period the whole monastic institution is constantly destroying and remaking itself. Reform integrates the system; by reform, the system realizes and maintains itself. Everywhere—in the Italian monasteries of the tenth century, Bobbio, Farfa, or the monasteries of Gaul, St. Bénigne, St. Denis, Montiérender— things move from extreme relaxation of the rule to extreme severity in its restoration. The Cluniac reform of the tenth century corresponds to the Benedictine reform under Charlemagne. If we are to believe Bernard of Hersfeld, whom we quoted above, the reform succeeded in placing Gaul under the strict observance of monastic discipline.

The reform was guided by an extraordinary man—St. Odilo. To understand him we must carefully strip away the pretty ribbons with which hagiography has wrapped him round.[6] He had succeeded St. Majolus, who was born in the diocese of Riez about 906, became abbot of Cluny in 948, and died in 994 after having reformed the abbey of St. Denis at the request of Hugh Capet. Odilo came from Auvergne, where he was born in 962. Elected abbot at the death of St. Majolus, he was throughout his long life (which ended in 1049) a man of high politics, as his predecessor had been. One might almost call him a statesman, not only be-

[6] On St. Odilo and Cluny around the year 1000, see G. de Valois, Le monachisme clunisien, Liguge, 1935, 2 vols.; also E. Amann and A. Dumas, Histoire de l'Église, Vol. VII, Paris, 1948, pp. 325ff.

9. South aisle, St. Etienne, Vignory. First half of eleventh century. (*Photograph:* Marburg.)

cause he had contact with all the sovereigns of his time but also
because of the part he played in what we call the building of the
West, especially through his connections with the two kings of
Navarre, Sancho and Garcia. St. Odilo gave form and substance to the great Cluniac enterprise of organizing Spanish
Christendom by introducting Western monasticism into the Mozarabic setting. Later, there will be the great pilgrim roads with
their landmarks, the churches, leading to distant Galicia and
Compostela. Without Cluny, Spain might well have preserved a
stronger and more lasting African flavor. Thus we are not dealing
with an obscure episode in annals of monasticism when we learn
of the mission of the monk Paternus, sent by Sancho the Great
to Cluny and charged on his return with the task of introducing
the rule at the monastery of San Juan de la Peña. Rather, this is
one of those notable facts that allow us to judge St. Odilo's wide-
ranging activities, which included relations with Stephen of Hungary, Casimir I of Poland, and even Emperor Henry II (Odilo was
present at the Emperor's consecration in 1014). Within France,
he performed his labors of reform with tireless courage and skill
—not only at St. Denis but at Paray-le-Monial (which the Count
of Châlon had given to Cluny in 999), at St. Flour, at Thiers, at
Saint-Sauveur of Nevers, at Charlieu, and at Nantua; and these
are merely examples.

He was one of those men of short stature who look unimpres-
sive, but who are indestructible and have a soul of steel. Not that
he was insensitive; it is agreed that he must have been "high-
strung" in every sense, and even full of compassion, to judge by
his splendid remark: "If I must be damned, I would rather be
damned for my pity than for my severity." But he is born to wield
authority, and his commanding nature drives him to seek a power
that he will not allow to be contested. Tears at times soften the
live coals of his eyes. But first of all this Christian is a leader. In
a period when monasticism boasts of so many towering figures—
men like Abbon, William, Goslin, Morard—the abbot of Cluny
is beyond doubt the most energetic, the man whose apostolic la-

bors most directly and most strongly affect the new structure of Europe and the transition from the Carolingian to the Romanesque world.

The work of his auxiliary, William of Volpiano, abbot of St. Bénigne at Dijon, follows the same principles and is also of European scope.[7] William, an Italian, has surrounded himself with a number of his compatriots; he may have called upon a Lombardian team to rebuild his church and the lovely rotunda joined to its apse. We are best informed on his activity in Normandy, where he brought the reform to St. Ouen at Rouen, to Fécamp, and to Mont-Saint-Michel; but his work extends also to Lorraine, and in Italy to St. Ambrose in Milan, St. Apollinare in Ravenna, and the abbey of Fruttuaria. He is a strange man, of a hardness that is almost frightening, whose display of austerity and whose ostentatiously humble exterior and manners shocked certain of his contemporaries. The unhappy monks of this unbending saint knew no mercy. Men call him William of the Super-Rule, *Supra regula*. Glaber, whose Life of William—*Vita Guillelmi*—cannot be suspected of ill will, in very few words paints a picture of the life that his companions at St. Bénigne are leading: *mortificatio carnis et abjectio corporis ac vilitas vestium, ciborumque extremitas vel parcimonia*. Some of the monks, exhausted by privations, dressed in rags, and terrified by their superior's brutality, took flight. Can it be that such harsh treatment was needed to subdue the arrogant and the rebellious? The monk Hermangaud, who escapes and takes to the road to seek comfort and protection with Fulbert, bishop of Chartres—friend and pupil of Gerbert—impresses us rather as a poor frightened fellow at the end of his strength. It would surely be a mistake to construct a picture of the Cluniac reform only from matter such as this; and we must keep in mind the periodic crises of unrest and ferment that stirred the monks of the West.

[7] On William of Volpiano, see R. Glaber, *Vita Sancti Guillelmi* (Migne, PL, CLII, col. 667–720); W. Watkin, "William of Dijon. A Monastic Reformer of the early XIth century," *Downside Review*, 1934, pp. 520–544.

b. Nave and transept, St. Cyriaque, Gernrode. Second half of tenth century. (*Photograph*: Stoedtner.)

The Cluniac reform was directed against indiscipline and also against the curiosity of man's intelligence—one might say, against the life of the mind. The ancient authors are held in abhorrence throughout the tenth and most of the eleventh century. St. Odilo in a dream sees a beautiful vessel, out of which crawl snakes; the vessel is classical poetry. St. Majolus, while studying in his youth at the school of the bishopric of Lyons, had read ancient philosophy, "the lies of Vergil." Knowing the writings, he bans them from Cluny. He mutilates the manuscripts by cutting out and destroying profane passages. The terrors of the year 1000 are more or less a legend; Pfister warns us that we must give up another legend, that of the monks spending their nights copying the ancient authors to save them for posterity: "The only writings which they copy are those of the Church Fathers. In the tenth and eleventh centuries, classical authors have no worse enemies than the monks, especially those monks who had gone through the reform at Cluny." [8] Besides, this hatred of the classics is not the monopoly of the Cistercians. We need only to listen to the reply made by the pope's legate at the Council of St. Basle-de-Verzy, to reproachful remarks on the ignorance of John XVI—a reply stating that Plato and Terence and all the rest of these vermin of philosophers are magicians, clever at flying, swimming, and climbing trees. This extraordinary exchange is of considerable interest because it shows that on this question there are several schools of thought within the Church, and that not everybody thought of the classical authors as vermin, black magicians, serpents oozing from a lovely vessel—or generally, in the words of St. Odilo himself, as poisonous creatures.

Accordingly, if we consider only monastic life as a whole and the broad outlines of the Cluniac movement, we might conclude that there was a retreat from Carolingian culture, if not a systematic reaction against it. Let us add further that Cluny in the year 1000—the Cluny of St. Odilo—is not the Cluny of St. Hugh

[8] C. Pfister, *op. cit.*, pp. 3–13.

the Great, and still less the Cluny of Peter the Venerable, that splendid soul so rich in his subtlety, one of the soundest and most attractive figures of the twelfth century. A time will come when the monks of the great basilica, whose high altar Urban II consecrated in 1088, will cause the figures of the Arts and the notes of the plainsong to be carved on the capitals of the sanctuary. A wonderful abundance of images, ornaments, realistic representations, and monsters will then come to life in the stone of the churches of Burgundy, churches that harmonize with antiquity in their proportions, distribution of masses, and architectural ornamentation. Literature and music will be honored. Then another reformer will appear who, in keeping with the rhythm of monasticism, will violently rise against these vain luxuries of the mind. St. Bernard and the monks from Cîteaux will lead the Church back to a severity that strips it to the bone, to the purism of Christian renunciation.

This is not to say that around the year 1000 there are not monastic islands where literature is held in honor. Abbon of Fleury—we have earlier mentioned his struggle against the wave of millenarian terrors that ran through Lorraine—suffered from the narrow limits and the inadequacy of teaching in the school of his monastery, which contented itself with the first two skills of the trivium, grammar and dialectic, and the first of the quadrivium, arithmetic. He went off to Paris to ask famous masters, possibly Gerbert himself, for the necessary complement. It must have been in Paris that he came to know the Latin poets whom he occasionally quotes in his letters, and that he acquired that elegant Latinity which made him famous, the knowledge of astronomy which he committed to a treatise, and the practice with the abacus and the nine Arabic numbers that were the inspiration for his harmless little verse happily playing with assonances: *His abbas abaci doctor dat se Abbo quieti*.[9]

Abbot Abbon, abacus expert, thus describes himself as a disciple

9 Quoted by C. Pfister, *loc. cit.*, p. 12.

of Gerbert who, influenced by the Arab culture of Spain, had revived such studies. This mighty figure, who will soon demand our attention in greater detail, naturally brings to mind the Catalan setting which he had visited in his youth, the region whose vitality in the tenth century is extraordinary. The monks who built the first vaulted churches of the West—St. Cecilia of Montserrat, St. Mary of Amer, St. Stephen of Banyoles, St. Martin of Canigou—were also men made for authority and for the high adventure of the mind.

It is well known what an important role this ancient Carolingian province has played; founded by Charlemagne, it had at first been held in benefice by counts, imperial officials who, just as other officials elsewhere in the West, took advantage of the decline and crumbling of the Empire to make themselves hereditary counts and gradually achieve complete independence, until they reach the point where we see them refusing homage to Louis V. For more than four centuries the earldom of Barcelona would remain the property of the house of the founder of the dynasty, Winifred the Shaggy, first among the counts of the region, among whose peers were, for example, the Count of Besalù and the Count of Cerdaña. In the year 1000, Catalonia is just recovering from a fearful conflagration, one of the last successful campaigns of al-Mansur. The capture of Barcelona and the conquest of a large part of Catalan territory had not put an end to the brilliant monastic and feudal culture about which we read in the beautiful works of Nicolau d'Olwer; in fact, that culture had not even been seriously shaken. Before and after that year, we have information on the lively activity in the mountain abbeys, and in Gerbert's time we know of his excellent friends there, who remained loyal to him as long as he lived, and to his memory after he died. A document signed by Ermengol I, count of Urgel, son of Gerbert's first patron, Borrell II, count of Barcelona, and dated 1004, preserves his title of the time, calling him *gloriosum sapientissimumque papam Gerbertum*. In his priceless correspondence we meet one of his faithful, Miro Bonfil, bishop of Gerona and count of Besalù, a

cousin of Borrell. In 984 Gerbert asks him for a book on the multiplication and division of numbers. During the same years he
turned to Llobet, archdeacon of Barcelona (975–992), to secure
a treatise on astrology translated from the Arabic, which he uses
to write his own treatise on the astrolabe. These few facts suffice
to demonstrate the importance of the intellectual exchange in
which Catalonia, at the end of the tenth century, could serve as
intermediary between Muslim science and the West; we shall return to it when we come to study the mighty personality of
Gerbert. For the moment, we need to recall these facts in order to
form a rounded idea of monastic thought and civilization, because
the history of monasticism is generally silent on the matter.[10]

But we have other indications as well; they are many, and con-
vincing. The instruction given at Ripoll, of which we know from
manuscripts 46 and 74 in the Barcelona Library, was notably more
complete than that of St. Benoît-sur-Loire under Abbon, for it
included the complete cycle of the seven liberal arts. Nicolau
d'Olwer rightly stresses the importance of the Vergilian glossaries
and the commentators on Vergil in the Library of Ripoll.[11] This
is at a far cry from St. Majolus and St. Odilo, from vessels oozing
serpents and "poisonous" authors. This is no longer the darkness
after the brief Carolingian "renaissance," but the dawn of the
Romanesque world. These are the mountain abbeys where the
Romanesque vault is first made to rise over the nave; here Romanesque culture begins to take form—not merely by maintaining a
tradition, but by producing a literature that is full of life, and subtle to the point of supreme originality.

The abbots of the tenth century writing in Latin, seemingly

[10] On Gerbert's relations with Catalonia, see: F. Picavet, Gerbert, un pape phil-
osophie d'après l'histoire et d'après la légende, Paris, 1897, pp. 30–34; N. d'Olwer,
in La Catalogne à l'époque romane, Paris, 1932, pp. 186–189, which sums up
his study Gerbert (Silvestre II) i la cultura catalana del segle X, Estudis Catalans,
1910, Vol. IV, pp. 332–358.
[11] N. d'Olwer, "Les glossaires de Ripoll," Union Académique internationale,
Bulletin Du Cange, 1928, pp. 137–152, and "Un glossaire de Virgile et de Juvenal,"
ibid., pp. 104–113.

lost among the rocks and gravel of the landscape that surrounds them, are in fact men of high sensitivity. One would expect them to have left to us some beautiful and crudely fashioned lives of saints, a hagiography of epic and rough outlines. Far from it; they are the most delicately skillful lovers of words, making splendid use of their glossaries to discover in them beautiful and difficult expressions. In short, they are a salon of literary artists. Cesari, or Caesar, was such a one, the abbot of Montserrat and pseudo-bishop of Tarragona, almost a monastic Tigranes of the tenth century. Nicolau d'Olwer quotes a letter he addressed in 970 to John XIII: it speaks of roses and of palms, the splendor of the starry sky, luminaries of virtue, the gentle bonds of sweetness, the heavenly throne.[12] We are entitled to ask ourselves if these influences are not an echo of contemporary Arab lyricism—which would in no way diminish, but on the contrary would enhance, the interest of this curious literature. In fact, these are the intellectual mannerisms peculiar to certain virtuosos who have gained a following, founded a school. Certain ones among them even seem to Hellenize, but in a most singular way: in their dictionaries they chose words of Greek origins, or rather words found in Priscian, source of the earliest medieval humanism, and in the glosses. This fact explains the form of two important acts of consecration, of Cuxa (974) and of Ripoll (977), both from the overly cultivated pen of Miro Bonfil. The same totally artificial taste for Greek is displayed by a certain Peter, a subdeacon who, in 1010, signs himself in Greek, but informs us with candor that he is ignorant of that language: *Petrus ὑποδιάκονος scripsit, quamvis incultus graeco sermone.*[13] Between 989 and 1009, we know of a judge in Barcelona called Oruç the Greek; whether the nickname is due to his knowledge, or perhaps to some travels he had made, we do not know.

These, to be sure, are weak traces. But they are not negligible. They round out the picture of a world which is in many respects

12 N. d'Olwer, *La Catalogne à l'époque romane*, p. 193.
13 Quoted by N. d'Olwer, p. 195.

profoundly different from the monastic world of Cluny and which anticipates and prepares the next development of Romanesque culture. Thus the traditions and the spirit of the monastic life show profound differences, depending on whether we study the life in the communities of Ireland, or on the continent as it was influenced by the Cluniac reform, or finally in the counties of the *Marca Hispanica*, where there had emerged certain forms that were to be of great importance for the future of Romanesque civilization, and where the abbots of the mountains, with their charming excess of literary verbalism, were moving in directions wholly opposite to the Cluniac destruction. But was the great monastic civilization of the Carolingians in fact dead? It would seem, on the contrary, that the restoration of the Empire by Otto the Great had given it new strength. To the Ottonians, just as to Charlemagne, the Empire is not just a political structure—it is an attempt to reawaken the past and the Roman spirit. That movement reaches its peak, its most intense moment, under Otto III, in the year 1000, but it runs ahead of that moment in certain quarters such as St. Gall and Reichenau and in women's convents such as Gandersheim and Quedlinburg, whose abbesses were two imperial princesses. Gandersheim is where the nun Roswitha began work on her epic poem *De gestis Ottonis I imperatoris* (962), and we know that she is also the author of Latin comedies more or less strongly inspired by Terence—Terence who is often mentioned during this period, together with Vergil, as a formidable prince of magicians, and who yet was read and appreciated in a convent in Germany by a woman of brilliance, herself a gifted writer.[14] Her drama written in a convent has surely a certain similarity with our own tragedies by college students. Yet there is something more: Roswitha knows life, the world, and love, down to the disorders and vagaries of sensuality. At Gandersheim, the nuns even played "politics" on the occasion of a celebrated litigation. In

---

[14] Roswitha (or Hrotswitha), *Carmen de gestis Ottonis I imperatoris* (*Mon. Germ. Hist., in usum scholarum*, Hanover, 1930); cf. A. Fliche, *Histoire du moyen âge*, Vol. II, *L'Europe occidentale de 888 à 1125*, Paris, 1885, pp. 225ff.

short, we are here dealing with an extremely lively group, whom the *Consuetudines* of Cluny had not yet sunk into the monotony of strict observance. Pirenne is quite correct in saying that Charlemagne has left a deep impression—but only in Germany, because the West is trying to discover itself, and to grow, in different directions, by different experiments. An abbot like Bernward is a Carolingian abbot, and his churches at Hildesheim are strictly Carolingian.

It would be a mistake to set up an impenetrable line of demarcation between the regular and the secular monks, or at any rate between the abbots and the bishops. A great abbot can be made a bishop. The archbishopric of Lyons was offered to Odilo—who, incidentally, declined it. Gerbert was abbot of Bobbio before he became archbishop of Reims and later of Ravenna. Goslin, abbot of St. Benoît-sur-Loire, was archbishop of Bourges. Abbot Bernward was bishop of Hildesheim. We could cite other examples, and add that in France the monastic fiefs remained attached to the bishoprics until the end of the *ancien régime*. The chapters of the canons constitute small congregations, and often very strong ones, held tightly together by a community of interests and even, to a degree, by a community of life. During a period when the seignorial regime is in its full flower, the abbeys and the chapters are feudal seigniories that own lands and serfs, and enjoy rights, privileges, and immunities. But whatever the political activities of the abbots of Cluny were, a bishop of the year 1000 is more directly involved in the life of secular business than they were. He resembles the lay feudal lords, especially when he comes from an illustrious family, as was frequently the case, and represents that family's pretensions, needs, and authority in his relations with the other prelates and with the reigning power. A bishop of the year 1000 may be a saint, but he is above all a baron. It is enough to recall the names of two archbishops of Reims, Hincmar and Adalberon, to realize the extraordinary role they played in the political history of ancient France; we recall the role Adalberon played in the dynastic revolution which in 987 took the crown from the Carolingians to place it on the head of a duke of Francia, Hugh Capet. But a special place must be given to those bishops who organized the territories newly conquered for Christianity, often according to quite different, even contrasting, ideas: Pilgrim of Passau, who organized the Germanism of Bohemia, and St. Adalbert, one of the most lyrical and most heroic figures of the Church in those days, a man whom we shall meet again in the court of Otto III.

Let us look more closely at one of the bishops of the century, one of those men of action of whom we have spoken. Bruno of Roucy, bishop of Langres, is well known to archaeologists, because the dates of his episcopal reign give us a chronological basis for an interesting church of the year 1000, St. Vorles in Châtillon-sur-Seine. However, he has a place in history on other grounds, at the time when Robert the Pious, King of France, on the death of Duke Henry, his uncle, in 1002, sets out to conquer Burgundy in order to uphold his rights as nephew and his royal title against the pretensions of the Count of Mâcon. Otte-Guillaume, whom Henry had adopted.[15] The issue was whether Burgundy would remain Capetian or become more or less imperial territory. Otte-Guillaume is an adventurer in the grand style, of Italian descent through his father Adalbert whose ephemeral kingship of Italy was destroyed by Otto the Great. His claim to Burgundy is only through his mother, who descended from an ancient count of Mâcon. A man of vast property in Franche-Comté, firmly entrenched in his maternal fief, Otte-Guillaume is supported by men like William of Volpiano and Bishop Bruno. The latter is quite naturally the king's enemy. He is Otte-Guillaume's brother-in-law through his sister Ermengarde; besides, bishoprics are of small importance to Robert the Pious in his political dealings. We should perhaps recall also that Bruno is a Carolingian prince. His grandmother is Gerberga, daughter of Henry I, King of Germany, and by her second marriage the wife of Louis IV—the queen, we

11. South aisle of choir, St. Michel, Cuxa. Second half of tenth century. (*Photograph:* Archives Photographiques.)

remember, to whom Adso abbot of Montiérender dedicated his *Libellus de Antechristo*. Bruno's diocese is in fact one of the large feudal estates which, side by side with the ducal domain proper, and under the duke's suzerainty, make up the duchy of Burgundy. He has important *pagi*, not merely that of Langres but those of Dijon and of Tonnerre and many others, often under beneficiary counts, his vassals. Such is the powerful territorial arsenal that the bishop of Langres in the year 1000 rules from his mountain top— from the upper valley of the Marne and the desolate plateau whose winters are so inclement, to the upper valley of the Seine, smiling, fertile, agreeable to man, in the countryside of Châtillon. Langres, on its jetty-head, is today the farthest outpost of Burgundy; but in those days, to go by the division of dioceses and archdiaconates, Troyes, Sens, and Provins were still Burgundian lands. Be that as it may, the man who then held Langres and extended his authority on one side to Dijon, and on the other to Tonnerre, was a lord of no small stature. Bruno of Roucy resisted for a long time. A diploma of 1006, quoted by Pfister, informs us that the royal authority was recognized in Burgundy, but the bishop of Langres had not submitted to it, and the abbot of Bénigne remained faithful to him despite Robert's urgent solicitations. Incidentally, it seems that the abbot's dominant character trait had not escaped the bishop's attention; in a low voice, the latter had remarked to one of his neighbors at an assembly that this ostentation of humility and virtue might be a weakness. Bruno died on January 31, 1016, and was replaced by Lambert, by virtue of a trade which gave Dijon to the king of France; and on the third of November of the same year, the church of St. Bénigne was consecrated.

Not all the bishops of the year 1000 are of royal lineage, as is Bruno of Langres, grandson of Gerberga, or Goslin of Bourges, bastard of Hugh Capet. Not all of them are as crude. His superior point of view, together with his flexibility of character, accounts, as we shall see, for the spectacular rise of a little monk from St. Géraud in Aurillac, a man from Aquitaine without high birth or fame—Gerbert. The Ottonians, whose client he was, would cover him with their favors and raise him even to the Papacy; we thus find him as Adalberon's successor on the see of Reims, which he had to hold against violent opposition, before he occupied the see of Ravenna, which he soon left for the papal throne. He is not a baron; he is a great lord of the mind, a friend of those "magicians" of past times who caused such horror to St. Odilo, a political mind combining many gifts in a mutually beneficient harmony—a bold vision, a sense of true greatness, together with that unidentifiable philosophical penetration and *amor fati* which are the mark of heroes or of sages. He is the hinge of two worlds, the Islamic East and Christianity, and of two eras, the Carolingian Middle Ages and the Romanesque Middle Ages. He deserves close study. But we had to mention his name here, side by side with those of his Catalonian friends, and with Miro Bonfil, bishop of Gerona. If the value of a civilization indeed lies in the diversity of the human specimens it produces and brings into play at any one time, then a period is surely not mediocre which gives to the Church St. Adalbert, Bruno of Roucy, and Gerbert of Aurillac.

But while they were strong personalities, did not the bishops lack that powerful single-mindedness which distinguishes Cluniac monasticism? Are they not divided in their interests? Had not baronial feelings broken their cohesion, by limiting the scope of their activity? What role could they have played in the building of the West? Among the multitude of facts which the history of the councils toward the end of the tenth century offers to our attention, historians have rightly stressed those that tend to prevent or at least limit the seignorial wars. It may be said that war is the normal condition of the century, not just between one power and another but between one lord and another. Since the public order is no longer guaranteed by a regulatory power, every man pursues his own pretensions or satifies his own desires by force of arms. The seignorial system implies seignorial war; neighbors kill each other, and that is called war. A large part of the efforts of the Capetian kings was devoted to limiting the brigandism of the lords—a century-long struggle which we see with extraordinary

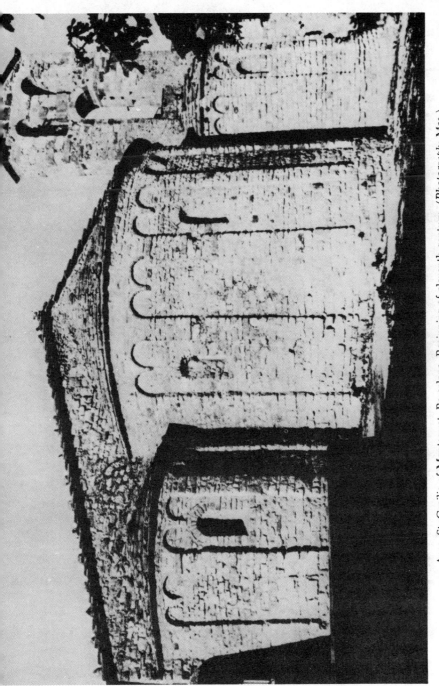

12. Apse, St. Cecilia of Montserrat, Barcelona. Beginning of eleventh century. (*Photograph:* Mas.)

clarity in the mid-twelfth century at the Grand Sessions of Auvergne. The Church of the year 1000 had labored toward the same end with remarkable consistency. In 989 and 990, the councils of Charroux and of Narbonne did no more than condemn seignorial war in principle. But in the same year as the latter council, the synod of Puy went a great deal farther; bishop Guy of Anjou established a technique of repression, by creating a police force "designed to prevent the breaking into churches, the theft of horses, the use of foreign labor in benefices or freeholds for the construction of castles, and so on." The purpose of these "peace associations" proposed in 997 by the Council of Limoges, and by the Council of Poitiers in the year 1000, was to revive the idea of the rule of law, and beyond that to create a force in the service of that rule—to band together in order to impose peace on the feudal brigands who devastate each other and crush the population. In 1027, the synod of Tuluges in Rousillon forbids fighting on Sundays; this prohibition is the beginning of the "Truce of God." But we feel that the prelates of the year 1000 had greater design than this Sabbath respite which is, after all, only a poor compromise. And it is interesting to note that this constructive movement, this reaction against one of the effects of the dissolution of the Carolingian Empire, takes its start in the center of France and spreads to the southwest and south, to Aquitaine, to Catalonia—those regions, that is, which become the foundation of Romanesque civilization.

Thus, while the monastic reform restores order in the cloisters by strictest discipline and by the surrender of the luxuries of culture, the bishops, by other means and in other fields, also attempt to restore order by building peace.

III

Of equal importance to the future of Europe are the political events of the year 1000. Their common characteristic is that they illuminate like beacons the great expansions and mass movements. In the northwest, these movements recall the invasions of the fifth century; they go hand in hand with the conversion of the maritime regions of Germany that had so far remained pagan. In the south, the reconquest and Westernization of Spain proceed at a slower pace but, from that moment on, with a continuity that nothing will interrupt again. In France, the Capetian monarchy, following feudal methods, embarks upon the century-long work of unification which it must pursue against the resistance of the feudal lords. Germany, finally, in concord with a great pope, conceives the outlines of the dream of universal Empire that begins as it will end—like a romance, stripped of all reality.

We turn first to those regions of the North Atlantic which in the course of the ninth century have spawned so many troubles and disasters for continental Europe and the British Isles, through the Norman invasions. That first wave of Vikings is followed by a second, of fearful proportions, in the next century. The Danes gain their empire in the Baltic, and quickly extend it to England. From Harold Bluetooth to Svend, and from Svend to Canute, the progression runs unbroken. In the second half of the tenth century, the Danes seem to be everywhere; a hundred years before (859) we meet them in the heart of Navarre, in Pamplona, and in many other places; under Harold (950–986) they establish that power, at once stable and mobile, which, resting firmly on the maritime bases torn from the feeble hands of England's Saxon kings and the anarchy of the Irish chieftains, keeps those loose political formations at its mercy. A ring of Danish settlements established in countless harbors, on small and middling islands, and at the mouths of rivers paralyzes all activity or takes a toll of its profits. These bases serve alike for war and piracy before they become commercial depositories. What drove the Danes on was more than the need to sell their fish and their iron swords; these cruel sailors were impelled by the sea nomads' instinct and the lust of burning, killing, and stealing. But just as they progressed from the period of raids to that of fixed settlements, so they proceeded from a condition of fragmentation, an organization of small pirate bands under a chief, small ocean kingdoms scattered across vast spaces, to the foundation of a sort of empire. It is re-markable, furthermore, that their apparent greatness coincides with their decline, and that when they become attached to the soil they lose their drive.

Christianity had made slow headway among the Danes since the middle of the tenth century. On January 2, 948, Pope Aga-petus II attaches three bishoprics—Schleswig, Ribe, and Aarhus —to the metropolis of Hamburg. We do not know the date of Harold's conversion. That he was baptized is certain, as were his wife Gunhild and his son Svend. He builds the cathedral of Roskilde, dedicated to the Trinity. We would gladly know more about this Nordic Christianity, superimposed on a Bronze Age civilization, ancient sun myths, and the primitive religion of the Germans. The Norse chiefs who enter Christianity do not leave their beliefs and instincts at the sanctuary door. Under the mod-ern, Christian surface, a thick substratum of human archaism will long remain. Svend himself would unleash a violent return to the gods of the past, much as occurred years earlier in Northumber-land. Yet these uncertain Christians fit into the new framework. The decisive fact for the Danes, as for the Norwegians, is that the structure of the Church is superimposed on the organization of the old society; the conversion of Olaf I (Olaf Tryggvesön) takes place around 995, that of the Swedes in the year 1000.

The summer of that year sees the great sea battle at Helsingborg which gives the Danes control of the Baltic Sea and at the same time secures their rear, so that they can safely pursue their opera-tions in England. The Danes and Swedes are on one side; the Norwegians and a Slavic people, the Wends, are on the other. Svend is in command of the former, Olaf is at the head of the op-posing forces. Olaf had served the Danes in England for a time, then had returned to Norway to become king in place of Haakon. He was conquered and killed in battle. In the division of the spoils, the Danes receive southern Norway, their allies the duchies of the Trondheim region. It might seem that this is a mere episode, strik-ing enough but remote and secondary, in the warfare among populations. But in fact the events of the year 1000 made possible the Danish conquest of England, and also those great expeditions which in the end broke the resistance of the Saxon King Ethelred —the expedition of 1009 led by the Vikings of Jomsburg, the expedition of 1010 (notable for the Danish victory of Ringmer and the payment of an enormous tribute), and finally the expedition of 1013–1014 which ends in the capture of London and Ethelred's flight to Normandy.

Why did Ireland escape England's fate, why did she not become Danish? In Ireland, anarchy was practically endemic. The clannish spirit of the Irish caused the total fragmentation of authority. In the middle of the tenth century, the Scandinavians held Cork, Waterford, and Limerick, where they had established small, very solid principalities with splendid naval bases. Everything suggests that the barbarian conquest will proceed successfully. An energetic and lucky chieftain manages to stop it dead. Brian and his older brother Mahon, the kings of Munster of the North, the Thomond, for many years fought epic battles to extend their power and maintain themselves, both against the Danes and against their own Irish partisans. Mahon disappears from sight in 976. In the year 1000, Brian has almost completed his task. Now fifty-nine years of age, he has beaten the Danes and their allies and is master of all southern Ireland. He is the acknowledged chief of all these chiefs without discipline, he wields the power, and in 1002 he assumes his title as successor to the *ard-ri*, Malachy II. Thus begins a splendid reign of twelve years which ends with his death in a fresh victory over a coalition of Scottish and Scandinavian chieftians at Clontarf (1014). Ireland is to lose her independence not so much by the fresh enterprise of pirates, traders, or colonists from Denmark, as by internal discord; but that will happen only in the twelfth century, after the Anglo-Norman invasion.

In our attempt to understand the events of which the years 1000–1002 were in some way the turning point in northwestern Europe, we notice that the basic anarchy of the barbarians tends to set up more stable establishments than it had done in the past. In the first Viking wave, in the ninth century, the sea adventurers in their long boats of the Oseberg type went abroad without any great political designs. The second wave, in the tenth century, leads them to conquer England; before that conquest and as a necessary first step, they had achieved unification in the Baltic, where the battle of Helsingborg assures the Danes of victory. They are aided by two totally opposite forces. The first is the preservation of the barbarian traditions and virtues in all their purity. The famous fortress of Jom, or Jomsburg, on the Oder appears to have been the center of this preservation, and of training; the Vikings of Jomsburg were called on for support in emergencies; Jomsburg was the place where young Canute was hardened, and the place that kept up the high intensity of the Viking drive. The second force is Christianity, which by and by accustomed them to other structures than those of a feudal society of pirates. A strange and battered Christianity it was; I have referred to the pagan reaction under Svend. Fifteen years after the death of Tryggvesön, who was baptized in England, another catechumen of the English clerics, named Olaf the Saint, tried to impose his faith on Norway. He had returned there to make himself king, taking advantage of the difficulties which Canute encountered in the early days of his reign; Olaf's absolutism provoked a revolt. The cathedral of Nidaros had not sunk beneath the shadow of the gods of yore. But we know what Canute meant to the Church. The combination of those two forces, the Viking drive and the constructive power of Christianity, aided the conquering Viking spirit in founding an empire. But, spread across the vastness of an icy sea and lacking inner unity, the empire later fell apart. The true and enduring foundation was the conquest of England by William in 1066. It remained for the Normans of Normandy, steeped in the continental disciplines by a century and a half of French living, to establish Western order permanently in England. But on the Bayeux Tapestry, made in commemoration of the expedition of 1066, there has come down to us an almost obliterated historic undercurrent, the memory of the great battle of the year 1000, at Helsingborg.

We turn now to the other extreme outposts of the West, to that Iberian world where since the closing years of the eighth century another struggle has been going on—the struggle between Christians and infidels, between the world of the Mahgreb and the small, insecure kingdoms clinging to the mountains of the Asturias and the southern foothills of the Pyrenees. The problem posed in the north in the year 1000 is whether the peoples of the sea are able to unite and to establish lasting settlements as they join the Christian community. The problem in the south is whether Spain will be African or European territory. No moment has ever been more critical than the years 997 and 1002. It looks as though the Christians will be swept from the peninsula forever by the victories of al-Mansur. He was an Arab of the finest, hardest metal, a military leader and a statesman; with the title of Hadjib, he was the true master of the caliphate of Cordova under Hisham II, the weak successor of al-Hakam. In 985 or 986 he takes possession of Barcelona, to lose it two years later to Count Borrell. In the years 987–988 Coimbra, Zamora, and Leon fall to him. In 997, the fall and destruction of Compostela echoes throughout Europe. The wave that carries al-Mansur threatens to engulf Spanish Christendom forever. In 1002 the threat is more terrible than ever with the "Canales en La Rioja" campaign that carries still other fortresses, still other monasteries, among them San Millan. But al-Mansur is spent, his destiny is flickering, nearing its end. We are told that when he had become weakened by sickness he had his men carry him to battle in a litter. He dies in that same year at Medinaceli, either from a wound received during a close victory won by the Christians, or from his sickness.

And then it seems as though history suddenly turned about. At no time has it been more evident that a man counts in the affairs of man. The man who disappeared had carried on his strong shoulders the burden of an empire. He falls, and the empire crumbles. The vast political structures of Islam are still more fragile than is

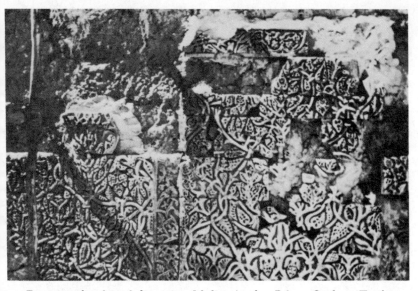

13. Fragment of sculptural decoration, Medina Azzahra Palace, Cordova. Tenth century. (*Photograph*: D. Fossard.)

the delicate architecture of their wood carvers and stonemasons
with its lacework of abstract ornament. Not that Hisham's successor was a weakling. On the contrary, his hardness, called ty-
ranny by the Berbers, provokes them to rise against him. With
the assistance of the Count of Castile, they carry Cordova in 1009.
From that time on the caliphate falls apart into principalities of
second rank, by a process analogous to the decay of the Carolingian
Empire. Islam will of course still achieve brilliant successes on the
peninsula, even see periods of splendor. It will resist for nearly
five hundred more years. But from 1002 onward it is on the retreat; and Christian Spain, her forces swelled with contingents
from the north, carries forward the reconquest begun in the second half of the eighth century by certain Visigothic noblemen
who had escaped from the disaster that befell their monarchy. At
the death of al-Mansur, another man arises who will put his stamp
on the events to come—the king of Navarre in the year 1000,
Sancho Garcia III, Sancho the Great. The very weakness of the
kings of Leon favors him, no less than the weakness of the caliphate. He takes advantage of it to enlarge his power; under his
reign appear the first outlines of a unity which seems to give
sanction to the ambitious title he assumes in certain documents
—*imperator Iberorum*—but which will be undone in the division
of his succession. His influence on his neighbor beyond the Pyrenees, Sancho Guillaume, Duke of the Gascons, is stronger than
that of the duke's nominal suzerains, the duke of Aquitaine and
the king of France. Finally we have seen him making an appeal to
Cluny, whose monks and whose rule he established in San Juan
de la Peña. By this act, no less than by his victories, he turns his
states into a solid base of Romanesque civilization, fully as important as the ancient *Marca Hispanica*, whose count in the year
1000, Romon, successor of Borrell since 993, is an equally tough
antagonist.

From now on we can discern the trend of the great historical
labors which are performed, on various levels, between Spain
and the West. Before the year 1000, the chiefs of the little moun-

tain kingdoms that had arisen from the resistance of Pelagius and his companions, uphold the old Visigothic traditions, though there are certain relations to Carolingian circles, as some churches of a type common to the Loire region of France (Germigny-des-Prés) and to the Asturias (San Miguel de Lino) tend to show. In the province of Barcelona, founded by Charlemagne, an original and brilliant civilization grows up during the tenth century, known to us through its accomplished Latinists and its builders; we shall see these builders raise their vaults over walls decorated on the outside with blind arches and fillets that are the heritage of a long Mediterranean past. This art is destined to spread north of the Pyrenees, while the rest of Christian Spain seems to have disregarded it completely. Of these two worlds that are so different, it may well have been the Mozarabic civilization that furnished a principle of unity—a unity exceedingly subtle, for the monuments of that civilization, its churches and manuscripts, are themselves very varied; but they are found over a vast territory that even includes Catalonia, and both kinds express a certain harmony between Christian Spain and Muslim Spain. They represent what is most remarkable and most original in the Iberian Christianity of the tenth century. Once the year 1000 has passed, this hybrid civilization survives only in a few isolated places. On the other hand, we then see emerging a double movement; the Spain of Sancho the Great and his successors welcomes the monks of Cluny, the knights of Poitou and Burgundy; and in the second half of the fifteenth century, wandering teams of architects and sculptors work on both sides of the Pyrenees. Then the Iberian world and the world of the Romanesque are joined harmoniously within a community of equally rich resources. But while it is important to take note of the retreat of Islam, and the advance made by its opponents, it is no less important to recall that Spain, now definitively joined to Europe, maintains its contacts with Islam—that it is thoroughly imbued with Islam and radiates its influence. We have seen that in the culture of the seafaring peoples Odin clashes with Christ, the Sagas clash with Christ, the culture of the

14. Wood carving, from Urnes church, Norway. First half of eleventh century. (*Photograph*: F. Henry.)

Bronze Age with the young cultures of Germany of the Ottos and of Saxon England, so also Iberian culture has a double tenor, but one which is retained much longer. Rising upon the powerful foundations of its Iberian, Phoenician, Greek, Greco-Roman, and Visigothic past, it is both the promontory of the West and the extreme spearhead of a vast wave from the East. This contradiction constitutes its greatness in the interplay of the Middle Ages and modern times.

The rest of Europe and particularly Capetian France, lying between these two battle fields—the Baltic and the North Sea on one side, the southern foothills of the Pyrenees on the other— seem in the year 1000 to enjoy a lasting stability. Indeed, the political revolution which in 987 installed the house of Robert the Strong in place of the last Carolingians, was to assure the country a remarkable dynastic continuity, which allowed a like continuity of political action. But the system that alienated territories from the royal domain would steadily reduce the sovereign's power, until the day came when another "reconquest" from the hands of the great feudal lords restored to the Capetians an authority founded on the crown possessions. Just like the France of the Carolingian kings in the ninth century, France in the year 1000 comprises three duchies, which are so nearly three kingdoms that in contemporary documents they are so designated—*regna*. Each of these in turn—besides the duke's own domain, in which he wields authority directly—comprises counties that are likewise feudal estates, and whose importance waxes and wanes in accordance with their territorial gains through war, exchange, inheritance, or marriage. It is a complex system of power within power, in which the unity imposed by the duke leaves room for enclaves and for movement. We shall understand the drama of the Carolingian monarchy in the tenth century if we recall that in that period two of the three duchies, and even all three, can be vested in a single authority that is not the king's. The point is that the Carolingian princes, despite the clear signs of the times, conceive of these divisions and subdivisions as a kind of administrative system inherited from the organization of the Empire (a character it retained much longer in Germany), while the dukes and counts are in fact no longer functionaries but landholders, with the duke placed above the other landholders and interposing his suzerainty between the vassals and the king. Hence the term *regnum* betrays not a false stress but what is almost a historical reality. If the Carolingians perished even though they were energetic, even though they were adroit, it was because they no longer stood on their own soil. And if the Capetians in the course of the eleventh century endangered the survival of the French monarchy, it was because they dismembered, or allowed the dismemberment of, their feudal foundation.

Under Robert the Pious matters have not yet reached that point. Among the three duchies—France, Burgundy, and Aquitaine—the royal house is the hereditary holder of the duchy of France, with a domain, the personal property of the duke and king, centered in the region called Île de France and the county of Paris. Thus France in the year 1000 is simultaneously, and on three very different levels, a dukedom and a count's region.

The duchy of France stretches between the Scheldt and the Loire, in the country of ancient Frankish Neustria, whose name is sometimes given to it in the texts. The feudal states that compose it, and over which the duke is suzerain, are many and powerful: the county of Flanders, to varying degrees under German influence; the counties of Arras, Amiens, Chartres, Tours, Blois, and the county of Anjou whose master in the year 1000 is the redoubtable Fulk Nerra, a canny and daring criminal, full of contrivances and fond of the surprise attack, who spends his life torn between his criminality and the fear of hellfire. The count of Normandy and the count of Rennes are beginning to assume the title of duke—duke of Normandy, duke of Brittany. Another important grouping develops around the county of Troyes, which is known as the "county of Champagne." But this short sketch in no way reflects the maze of secondary counties, or of the episcopal feudal structure, or of the interstitial network of viscounts and vicaries and castellanies with which the duke of France, and the other dukes as well as the counts, his vassals in Francia, multiply and strengthen the number of their supporters. The king, being a duke, profits from this diversity. He maintains himself in power by politics and war. His strength lies in the fact that the royal title vests in him an ancient and traditional moral authority, going back even before Hugh the Great and resting on the prestige of the Robertians. The name Neustria, used to designate the duchy, must not mislead us. But it is nonetheless a memory resting on some authentic reality, a certain community of the people beneath the divisions of the lords, to which Philip Augustus, after a period of disintegration, will restore the fullness of its political meaning. The Île de France will re-establish Francia if not the duchy, and Francia will establish France by restoring the equilibrium of the West that had been destroyed by the Anglo-Norman expansion. From the year 1000 onward it appears that the Loire, the duchy's southern border, is an axis of the kingdom. Here lies the explanation for the importance of Orléans; and archaeology finds confirmation in the rapidity with which, toward the end of the tenth century, a new type of church multiplies along the river.

We have referred earlier to the territorial structure of the duchy of Burgundy, whose counties are staggered along the Seine and the Yonne, the Loire and the Saône. It is a political formation utterly distinct from the county of Burgundy, the Franche-Comté, and the kingdom of Burgundy, a survival of the ancient portion of Lothair which extends—with enclaves—along the left bank of the Saône and the Rhône and includes the Jura and the western parts of what is now Switzerland. This rich duchy, studded with towns and abbeys, covers a landscape facing in two directions; one side descends toward the Mediterranean, the other toward ducal France. The moment we pass from one to the other southward, crossing the watershed between them at Blaisy, we step into a different world; our eyes meet the horizon of a different sea under other skies. At that time, the duchy of Burgundy is held by a Capetian prince, Henry the brother of Hugh Capet, uncle of

Robert the Pious. When he dies in 1002, the pretensions of Otto-William, the Italian son-in-law of Henry, force Robert to make war, in his double capacity as king and as the natural heir. Long and hard-fought, skillfully conducted by the Capetians, the war does not truly come to an end until the death of Bruno de Roucy, bishop of Langres. The duchy then becomes the domain of two of the king's sons, first Henri and then Robert. The county of Dijon, taken from the bishopric of Langres, is henceforth the center and seat of a new power destined to involve the French monarchy in the gravest risks.

The same is true of Aquitaine, in consequence of the repudiation of Eleanor, daughter of Duke William X, by Louis VII, that curious political master stroke which for a time gave half of France to the English. The duchy of Aquitaine, called at times the "monarchy of the Aquitainians," deserves that title by virtue of its great size and unity. True, the duke of Gascony in the south is a most unreliable vassal, set apart from the rest of Aquitaine and from France by a profound difference in origin, customs, and language. Hostility occasionally rises to the point of violence, witness the murder of Abbon of Fleury, who came to take possession of the abbey of la Réole, attached to St. Benoît-sur-Loire (1004). We also recall the ties that bound Sancho William to the king of Navarre, Sancho the Great. The county of Barcelona, on the other hand, belongs directly to the crown; we see Borrell appealing to Hugh Capet at the time of al-Mansur's great invasion, and the king demanding first a formal guarantee of Borrell's loyalty, which the new king had good reasons to doubt. With these two reservations—the irreducible tumultuousness of Gascony, and the special situation of the *Marca Hispanica*, which, incidentally, is turning more and more toward Spain—Aquitaine stretches from the Loire to the Pyrenees, and includes the counties of Toulouse, Poitiers, Limoges, Haute-Marche and Basse-Marche, Auvergne, Périgord, and many others from which illustrious names have sprung. In the year 1000, the duke of Aquitaine is William V the Great, successor of William IV Fièregrace, count of Poitiers. He

15. Ruins of church, Limburg im Hardt. First half of eleventh century. (*Photograph:* Staatliche Bildstelle, Berlin.)

is a very powerful lord, worthy of wearing a king's crown as well as the golden band which he receives at the ceremony of his investiture at St. Martial of Limoges. It is said that he was tempted for a time by the crown of Italy, and that he had the wisdom to renounce it. This noble and exceedingly hard-fisted baron seems to have been a prudent and loyal vassal of the Capetian monarchy, receptive of the charms of friendship, a lover of literature and fine books. Canute gave him great pleasure by sending him a superb manscript from England. The event is an indication of a relationship which, reinforced by dynastic alliances, provides us with an explanation why St. Hilaire of Poitiers was built by an English architect, Gautier Coorland (1049). Aquitaine in the eleventh century—grown rich through the wealth of the West and especially the South, in contact with Islamic civilization, through the Spanish crusade, in touch with Burgundy (witness the foundation of the Tournusian priory of Sainte-Croix in Loudon)—Aquitaine is destined to be one of the great centers of Romanesque civilization; from the year 1000 onward we can discern it by the importance of its abbeys.

This kingdom composed of three duchies, of which one belongs to the sovereign, one to his uncle, and the third to his son, looks at first like a kind of cohesive imperial structure with the advantage of fronting on two seas, while Germany needs either the kingdom of Burgundy, long coveted by her weak prince Rudolf III, or else Italy, which the Italians themselves refuse to her, to gain access to the Mediterranean. But to hold the structure together a chief is needed, followed by a continuous line of chiefs; and equally necessary is a theory of monarchy. Who is the king of France in the year 1000? Not just a count of Paris and a duke of France, which is already a good deal, but the suzerian who is, in theory, recognized throughout the kingdom of the Franks. His power is elective and indivisible. But by associating their sons with the exercise of royal power, and causing them to be recognized and consecrated in the king's own lifetime, the first Capetians secured the crown to their own offspring with undivided authority.

Thus the Capetain revolution, like all others, tended toward hereditary dynasty. In July 987, Hugh Capet, elected at the assembly of Senlis, is crowned at Noyon. In that same year his son Robert, associated to the royal power, is crowned at Orléans.[16]

In the year 1000, Robert is thirty years old. He has succeeded his father, by right, in 996. We do not know whether he has already repudiated his wife Bertha, but the event seems firmly established by 1001. He had first been compelled to marry the woman whom he called "that ugly Italian," and whom he despised, Suzanne, daughter of Berenger, King of Italy, and widow of Arnulf, count of Flanders: there was indeed a need to tie that fief, threatened by German advances, more closely to the crown. It was a sad political union, and broke up at the end of the first year. Love would lead him to marry Bertha, widow of Odo, count of Chartres, Tours, and Blois; by a reversal of alliances, he would be led to uphold the interests of that family against Fulk Nerra. But Bertha was his blood relation, and in addition he was godfather of one of her children. Such marriage constituted a double crime, not so much in the eyes of the French episcopate as in those of the German Pope Gregory V,* who cast the bolt of his anathema. If Bertha was finally repudiated, it was no doubt because she failed to bear an heir to the dynasty. What legends there are about the excommunicated king, and the kingdom struck by interdict! Historic reality is totally different.

Robert the Pious deserves his name; like many other sovereigns of his time, however, he does not consider himself entirely acquitted of his duties as Christian just by attending services and founding churches. He had a warmth and gentleness that make him very attractive. But how can it be forgotten that this friend of the monks, in the course of his Burgundian campaigns, had made life extremely hard for the abbots of St. Germain of Auxerre and of St. Bénigne, and had resisted St. Odilo? How can

---

[16] On Robert the Pious, see especially Helgand, Vie du roi Robert (E. Pognon, op. cit., pp. 235–264), and C. Pfister, op. cit.
* In the French edition, the pope's name is erroneously given as Martin V.

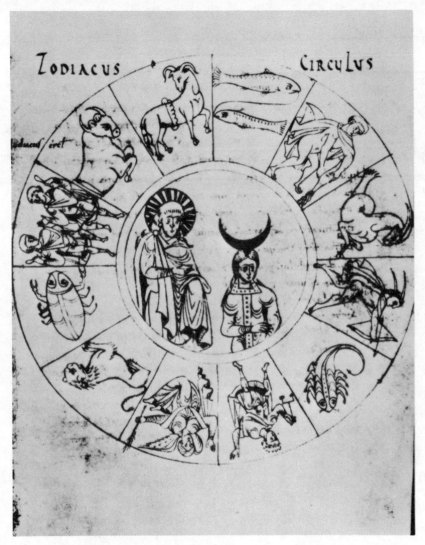

16. Zodiac, from Aratus' astrological treatise. Codex 250, St. Gall Library. Ninth century. (*Photograph*: Hurlimann.)

it be forgotten that he made clever use of his episcopate in politics, by trading bishoprics for territorial gains? No man took a more exalted view of his rights as overlord and his duties as king. His biographer, the monk Helgaud, has turned him into a mummy, and we must restore to him the vigor and drive he possessed in life. Perhaps Hugh Capet had been compelled to give up his predecessor's Lorraine policy in order to become king. Robert resumed that policy. He is not satisfied to maintain the shaky and complex structure of his suzerainty by constant warfare; he sees beyond the immediate interests of his lordship. On more than one occasion, he shows himself a true king.

This is the prince who has been described in so many words as a "nonentity" by certain historians who have allowed themselves to be misled by pious stories—stories which, by the way, have many human and charming things to say about him. It does not matter that he could not always control his third wife, Constance of Arles, whom he married in 1003. She was haughty, vain, and willful. She gave him children, and much bitterness. This sensitive and kind Neustrian had no aptitude to play the domestic tyrant that is normal on the Mediterranean. To the amazement of the people and the clerics he allowed his wife to set the tone at court. The southerners, specially the Aquitanians whom she brought with her, were sharply different from the people of the North. These encounters are in some ways extraordinary. The attendants of the new queen produced a shock from the very start. "They neglected arms and horses," says Glaber; "they had their hair cut halfway down their head; they were shaved like actors; they wore shameless boots and shoes. . . . All the French people, once so virtuous above all others, and even the Burgundians themselves, imitated these despicable examples." Abbot William rebuked the lords, and the chronicler asserts that he averted the danger. But it is important to know that the Romanesque world and Capetian society, still wholly Carolingian, were thus confronted. At any rate, there seem to be no signs that they fused, either in manners, in their language, or in their monuments.

Still, the equilibrium of the West will be brought about in France, or by means of France. In France proper, it will be brought about by the stability of the dynasty, the consistency of the monastic reform, the efforts of the clergy to neutralize or restrain feudal warfare, that agent of dissolution; it will be brought about above all by a geographical harmony that proves stronger than all human disagreements. France is the hearth from which the monks of Cluny, and later the lords of Poitou and Burgundy, will sally forth to Spain, bringing with them the forces that will serve effectively in the crusade of the Spanish reconquest. Soon the descendants of Norse pirates, who in Normandy had become settlers, vassals, and Christians, would establish that strong and lasting dominion over Great Britain which the Saxons and the Danes had been unable to maintain. The year 1000 already foreshadows new structures, with Svend in the Baltic and the North Sea, Sancho the Great in Spain, and King Robert in France. However uncertain their future may seem at that point, these are the trials and struggles that lead us to what the millenarians would have called a new age of the world—the Middle Ages. What role did the papacy play then? What role the Empire?

THREE

The Pope in the Year 1000

HOWEVER constant the recurrence may be of certain general phenomena in the life of history, however powerful the institutional framework inherited from the past, and however great the importance of certain collective movements in which the individual is swept along, a knowledge of human nature still remains indispensable to historical inquiry. Man not only stamps events with his individual abilities, purposes, and inclinations, he can also give them a direction and a shape—he can even determine them. The problem that raises special difficulties in the history of the Middle Ages in this still vague period separating the Romanesque world from that of the Carolingians—even in a region which, being the heartland of the West, already seems aware and alert, and animated by reflection—this problem is that man is difficult to grasp, and that in trying to define his character we are always in danger of missing the truth, or distorting it. Even when we are in possession of the most detailed biographies, we must begin by criticizing the biographer himself. And we often know men only by a few outward acts separated by long stretches of obscurity.

We have been able nonetheless to learn more than the name of a certain number of personalities of the year 1000. Men like Sancho the Great, William of Aquitaine, Odilo, Robert the Pious

—to mention only the leading characters—stand before us, not like shadows cast upon a wall by a vague light, but as living and complex beings—even when, like the reformer of Cluny, they are moved by a single thought which bends all their efforts to a single end. Thus we are able to discern that even though they are contemporaries, they belong to different ages: Svend the Dane, architect of Baltic unity, the Norwegian St. Olaf who wants to force his country to join the Christian community, and even the Irish chieftain Brian seem to emerge from the depths of a very remote past. The others are "modern men"—that is, men fully of their own times, men who shoulder the duties and perform the labors of their times, who organize monarchies, monastic orders, trading companies, and peace associations. Still others are fore-runners of a certain type of man that is still very rare, and of a new spirit.

Such a one was the Pope of the year 1000, Gerbert of Aurillac, who chose the name Sylvester II when he was elevated to the papacy.[1] We are wonderfully well informed about his life and work, by his own pen; a little information comes from his books, a great deal from his letters which reflect faithfully his plans— even his secret plans—and his ideas, his moods, and his friend-ships. Their elegant Latin not only shows him as the great scholar he was, but betrays with much charm and ease the working of a mind of the first magnitude and an uncompromising soul, driven not so much by ambition as by a nostalgia of greatness. As the teacher of an entire generation, he exercised a profound influence on his age. The very legend that surrounds him, and that portrays him as a prince of magicians in league with the Demon, only suc-ceeds in demonstrating that he was not a mere vague harbinger but himself a man of the Renaissance, an encyclopedic mind,

[1] On Gerbert, besides the essential source Richerus, *Historiarum libri IV*, ed. Pertz, in *Monumenta Germaniae*, 1833), see: A. Olleris, *Œuvres de Gerbert*, Clermont and Paris, 1867; J. Havet, *Lettres de Gerbert* (983–997), Paris, 1889; K. Schultes, *Papst Sylvester als Lehrer und Staatsmann*, Hamburg, 1891; F. Picavet, *Gerbert, un pape philosophe d'après l'histoire et d'après la légende*, Paris, 1897; F. Eichengrün, *Gerbert (Sylvester II) als Persönlichkeit*, Leipzig, 1928.

equally well equipped for scholarship and for action and high authority. The difficulties he encountered were caused, so to speak, by the fact that he lived before his time. The fact that he triumphed over them—that he even dominated his own fate—gives us the measure of his spirit. He began by being a kingmaker—he made the king of France, whose son he had been educating. In order to fulfill his destiny he met a young Emperor, a hero and a saint who died at twenty. The little monk from Aquitaine who had become Pope, and the son of the beautiful Greek Empress shared their dream of wresting the Holy Empire away from its narrow Germanic confines, and of resuming the work of Sylvester I and Constantine. If Otto III had been alive, would they have succeeded? It is not likely. But their very failure only enhances the nobility of these two great lives.

I

Gerbert is endowed with the gifts of his native Aquitaine, a Latin humaneness beneath the surface which is never totally suppressed, great liveliness and fervor and everything that goes with what is called a happy disposition. We know nothing of his family except that it was obscure, *obscuro loco natum*, says the chronicle of Aurillac, and that text is supported by a letter from Gerbert to Wilderode, bishop of Strasbourg, in which he states that he had been assisted neither by his birth nor by the possession of wealth: *nec genere nec divitiis adjutus*; the attempt to make him a relative of Ebrard, abbot of St. Martin of Tours, rests on a false interpretation of certain other letters. He was one of those poor and gifted children whom the abbeys and the bishops' schools were seeking out, and who at times were aided in their studies by generous individuals; he would encounter many such around his bishop's throne in Reims. He was educated from an early age at the monastery of St. Géraud in Aurillac, like so many other school children in those days, like the students of Abbon at St. Benoît-sur-Loire, just as Glaber was educated at St. Germain in Auxerre. The abbey of Aurillac was one of the important houses of Aquitaine. We know of its quarrels in the eleventh century with Sainte-Foy of Conques, which ultimately overshadowed it. His masters were the abbots Gerard and Raymond, and he remained warmly attached to them all his life. In this graceful soul, the memories of his monastic childhood retain great sweetness. Later at Reims, when he was already covered with honors, he had preserved and demonstrates his full affection for them. He sends them presents in the name of his archbishop Adalberon—and in the letter going with the present, not one person has been forgotten: he sends his greetings to Raymond, to Airard, and all the brothers. Still later, when he has been raised to the episcopacy, he asks for their prayers. Beneath his turns of phrase which are a little cloying—*dulcissime frater, amantissime*—there is a constancy of affection that will not be denied. He likes to say that he owes everything he knows to Raymond: Raymond has taught him grammar—which means Latin, a language no longer generally spoken but still the language of cultivated men, and of great public occasions. Hugh Capet, who knew no Latin, had to have an interpreter at certain political encounters. Knowledge of Latin was still the key to a clerical career. Raymond was an excellent teacher, to judge by the Latinity of his pupil, who was one of the most brilliant writers of the Middle Ages.

This human climate represents a striking contrast with the rigors of St. Bénigne and the rough discipline of Fleury, and we understand that it meant a great deal for Gerbert to have spent his tender years in such surroundings, and on the soil of Aquitaine which would define, and become the stage of, the first Romanesque culture. Equally important was his journey to the Spanish province. In 967, Borrell, son of Sunier Count of Urgel, succeeded Seniofred as count of Barcelona. On the occasion of his marriage he went to France and stopped at St. Géraud; at his request, the monks entrusted to him the pupil in whom they took the greatest pride, a student who had become their brother and dear friend. The count sent Gerbert to Hatto, bishop of Vich.

We took a look earlier at Catalan civilization and its literature, refined, somewhat complex, a little brittle and derivative. These Latinists and Hellenizers, at the end of the tenth century, move us because they differ sharply from the Cluniacs and their iron antihumanism. But that is only one facet of their intellectual life. Through Isidore of Seville, they maintained contact with the science of antiquity. In their company, and drawing from this spring, Gerbert no doubt deepened his knowledge of philosophy and theology. It has been noted that his definition of philosophy—*divinarum et humanarum rerum comprehensio veritatis*—is wholly Isidorian. In addition, he steeped himself in the sciences, which in those days meant arithmetic, surveyor's geometry, and astronomy. Was he acquainted with Arab science? Did he visit Cordova? That visit is one of the main elements of the legend of Gerbert the magician. Adhemar of Chabannes asserts that Gerbert was lost to the cause of science and philosophy—*causa philosophiae*. Ascelin of Laon applies to Gerbert the name of a king of Egypt, land of wizardry: Neptanabus. Around 1080, Benno accuses him of witchcraft, Sigebert of Gembloux (who died in 1113) of necromancy. Ordericus Vitalis (died 1141) reports Gerbert's interview with the Devil. William of Malmesbury, finally, gives us the entire romance. Gerbert has gone to Cordova to study the accursed sciences, fallen in love with the daughter of his Sarazen host, and eloped with her. The romantic story interweaves magic spells with Devil's ruses. But all these anecdotes are strung together very crudely. What remains is the plain allegation of Adhemar of Chabannes. Yet neither Gerbert nor his disciple Richerus, who abounds with priceless details of his master's education, makes the least allusion to the matter. We may say further that a journey to Cordova was not a simple matter in the tenth century; the troubles of John of Gorze, sent to the court of Abd-Al-Rahman at the time the latter also sent an embassy to Otto I (952), are sufficient proof. But was it absolutely necessary that Gerbert go to Cordova in order to establish contact with Muslim culture? Surely that culture was not at its most brilliant at this time, nor in this place, the Mahgrab: the great period of Avicenna and Avicebron had not yet come. But Cordova was a center of learning nonetheless. Certain important or interesting texts had been translated by the Jews. Gerbert's correspondence with his friends in Catalonia, two of whom he asks for copies of their books, speaks of a treatise on astronomy whose author he does not identify. He also desires a work by Leo the Wise or Leo of Spain. Though it is impossible to establish with precision what William of Malmesbury took over from these Judeo-Arab sources, I do not think we should entirely reject in William's gossip everything he tells us about the church organs, clocks, and celestial globes that Gerbert knew how to build or to have built by others. It is quite possible that during the decline of the art of mechanics in the West, Gerbert acquired a practical knowledge of it from Islam, the heir of the Byzantine "mechanics." In any event, let us remember from here on that in this century, when men's thought was almost invariably lacking in vitality because of its abstractness, Gerbert displayed a taste for the concrete, a sort of genius for craftsmanship that makes him akin to the men of the Renaissance. We readily understand what influence such a teacher would exercise later by his studies of astronomy, which employed the sphere to explain the movements in the sky. We find it difficult to say whether or not he was indebted to the Arabs for suggestions or examples in this matter. But this specific aptitude for working with his hands, which distinguishes him from the philosophers of his day, is altogether Gerbert's own. The same is true of his use of the abacus, and of his spreading the use of what we call Arabic numerals; while they are not originally Arabic, they were in general use in Muslim Spain.

Whatever the truth of the matter may be, Gerbert retained profound impressions from his stay in Catalonia, and remained as faithful to the friends he made there as he did to his teachers at St. Géraud. These are the friends to whom he writes asking for certain manuscripts: he begs Miro Bonfil, bishop of Gerona and count of Besalù, to send him the book of Leo the Wise on multiplication and division (984), and asks Llobet, archdeacon of Barcelona (975–992), for the treatise on astrology which he may have used in composing his treatise on the astrolabe. Many years later, when he had to leave Bobbio, his thoughts return to these circles which were dear to him and where he had faithful friends. He was tempted to settle there (at the end of 984 or the beginning of 985); Guarino, abbot of the Mozarabic monastery of St. Michael in Cuxa, urged him to do so. In a letter which betrays his indecision he asks for the disinterested advice of Abbot Géraud: "At times I dream of removing myself near to the Spanish princes, as abbot Guarino urges me, at other times I am turned from the purpose by the letters of Empress Theophano. . . ."

In March of 986 he is still vacillating between the imperial court and Spain, as we know from a letter to Abbot Nithard. We know besides that on the death of King Lothair he was appointed secretary of Queen Emma. Spain then offered him a retreat into wisdom, together with superb friends and the books he craved. Cuxa, which later would be the refuge of St. Romuald and of the doge Orseolo, would have made a worthy asylum for Gerbert. But destiny, as well as his own more or less overt inclinations, saved him for high position and the dangers of the active life.

Thus the ties remained strong that bound him to Catalonia even after his departure. He stayed there for three years, from 967 to 970. Before he returned to France—though not to Aurillac— Count Borrell and Bishop Hatto took him with them to Rome. They were going to Rome to ask the pope to make Vich an archbishopric, so that it might be separated from Narbonne, of which the bishop of Vich was a suffragan. This attempt is connected with the efforts of the counts of Barcelona, vassals of the king of France, to gain greater independence in their relation to the crown. Accordingly, when Borrell turned to Hugh Capet for aid and protection at the moment of al-Mansur's great invasion, Hugh insisted that before any military understanding could be reached the count would have to acknowledge his feudal duties. But the fall of Barcelona occurred in 987, while the papal diploma of John XIII, showing that the travelers were present in Rome, dates from

971. And that is the occasion when Gerbert began his relations with the house of Saxony, which were to exercise so deep an influence upon his life. The Pope and the Emperor took a liking to him, not only because of the extent of his scholarship, but surely because of his personal charm, which still touches us when we read his letters. The somewhat flowery geniality of these letters sometimes makes us marvel at his cleverness. But this clever man is also a master, and it is clear that he was prone to love—to love his spiritual fathers, his friends, his patrons, and later his pupils. In that crude age and amid those hard souls, the brilliant Aquitainian with his sweet disposition reminds us of the moral and intellectual grace of ancient Rome at her best, when the first rays of the Greek sun began to warm and soften Roman rigor. Scipio Aemilianus and Lelius would have liked him. In that Rome of his young days—a wholly feudal Rome, scene of those struggles which pitted against one another the barons of Latium, a lawless population, a vacillating papacy, and the Saxon Emperor—Gerbert is fully at home, more than any of them. It is said that he won his illustrious friends by his astronomy, by music, above all because he represented a type of man that had become extremely rare, or rather had almost completely vanished. The Emperor and the Pope urged each other to retain him in their close retinue—did not Otto I want to surround himself with outstanding scholars and men of letters, as Charlemagne had done? To restore the Empire—did that not mean also to restore imperial culture? Again, was not a man like Gerbert made for Rome, and for the papal court? Yet Gerbert followed neither of the two roads. It was due, perhaps, to a remarkable prudence; the Emperor soon died—and there was nothing more unstable than the churning papacy of the tenth century. All men of Gerbert's scope possess a hidden sense of their destiny. In any case, he considered himself weak in dialectics, and chose to go elsewhere to complete his education.

The episcopal school at Reims was then flourishing under the guidance of Adalberon (969–989). Garannus, archdeacon of that famous church, was in Rome, having been sent there by Lothair,

King of the Franks. Gerbert decided to leave with him. No doubt the Emperor paid for the expenses of the journey. On the way the two scholars taught each other what they knew. In mathematics, Garannus made good progress. But he had no head for music.

II

This is the beginning for Gerbert of the most fruitful, most real most effective period of his life: ten years of teaching and study, in the course of which the "brilliant subject" becomes himself a master, and strikes out upon an astounding political career.

The travelers reached Reims at the end of 972 or the beginning of 973—after Richerus had joined the Council of Mont-Notre-Dame in Tardenois, and Otto I had died (May 9, 973). Like other men of his time past their first youth, who did not hesitate to go back to school, so Gerbert—already widely known, already possessing the friendship of men in high places—became once again a student. But he was soon singled out by Adalberon, who entrusted him with the management of the school by naming him a scholastic or, to use an ancient title that sounds at once pedantic and naive—a scholiast. Once again we here see at work that same upward urge, operating with the same sureness, which earlier had touched the abbot Géraud, Count Borrell, Gerbert's Catalan friends, and finally John XIII and Otto I. The archbishop of Reims felt that a teacher who had gained such a reputation in Aquitane, in Spain, and in Italy was well suited to spread the reputation of his schools abroad. Adalberon, being a statesman, also appreciated at its full value the favor Gerbert had gained at the imperial court, where Otto II continued to show him the same kindness as had Otto I. All these are excellent reasons. But seen from the outside, by minds of small perception, of mediocre range, and forever confined to the lower regions, this splendid rise of a human being was bound to look suspicious. The enchantment of charm and superiority alone could not explain it. And what will it be later, when the intimate of the Devil will reap the highest honors and finally the supreme honor! Abbon's rancor is nothing but the jealousy of the academy. He is preparing to accuse Gerbert of sorcery.

We find ourselves here at the extreme opposite of Cluny, and on a plane much higher than that of the Carolingian civilization. Gerbert brings to the confines of Austrasia something that is not pure scholarship but a turn of mind, a way of thinking and of conveying understanding. It may be true that he was not one of those minds who burst upon the world with a sudden discovery, who cast a brilliant, concentrated light on some point of research. But he radiates a steady and pure light on every field of human knowledge of his times. He possessed this high gift, talent, which is as necessary to human progress as is genius, but is suspect and even hateful to the vulgar. Talent, for a teacher, consists above all in moving others to live and to love the subject of his teaching. Success, which is so odious to the pedants that they regard it as a mortal sin, here is the irrefutable testimony to superiority and effectiveness.

We know Gerbert's teaching, its form and its spirit, through the testimony of Richerus. He understood logic and mathematics, that is, the trivium of literary and philosophical instruction, and the quadrivium, that is, scientific instruction. The first of the liberal arts, the first branch of the trivium, is grammar, which is studied from the works of Donatus, Priscian, and Martianus Capella. The students who came to Gerbert already knew the rudiments. To use the phrase of Abbon's biographer, they were now qualified to swim the immense ocean of Priscian which at that time was thought of as the source of all knowledge of Latin. Next came dialectics, a science in which Gerbert had perfected himself while at Reims, and which included the study of the categories of Porphyrius, Boethius' works on logic, and Cicero's *Topics*. Nothing could be drier than such a discipline based on the analysis of the *quinque res*, gender, species, difference, properties, and accidentals, and the various forms of syllogism. Still, it was capable of loosening the mind, of making it more supple and training it, not for the exercise of critical judgment which rests on totally different principles, but for speed and subtlety in reasoning. Gerbert appears indeed to have understood it in this sense, transcending those definitions which to us today seem purely verbal; he took his students to a "sophist" who trained them in the peculiar gymnastics of discussion. Here we see coming to the fore Gerbert's preference for the concrete, which was characteristic of his teaching; we shall meet more examples as we proceed. What interests him is not notions and ideas as such, but the way in which they come to life in the mind. He makes use of those arid data in order to awaken the activity of the intellect, and to guide it. We must grant that they are arid—but they essentially constitute the medieval technique of thinking, which is far from negligible; and the development of an analogous technique, a dialectic of or speculation on pure forms, is in all likelihood at the root of Romanesque sculpture. Besides, when we read Gerbert's little treatise *Libellus de rationali et ratione uti*,[2] we shall understand its true meaning only by interpreting it as the play—an almost wholly "ornamental" play—of this mind. How can it be said that a reasonable being uses reason, since what is reasonable is necessarily contained in the use of reason? We must distinguish potential and act. The reasonable being is defined by reason, but does not always use it. This is an example of the problems Gerbert posed to his students, and which he solved for them with the most elegant subtlety. The *Libellus* may well be a "term paper," or a "sample lesson" which he wanted to preserve.

But it is generally agreed that the full measure of his originality is to be found, not in dialectic but rather in rhetoric—a field in which he stands out as a prince of the humanists. First of all, he abandons the manuals and returns to the sources. Which sources? The texts of the masters which he untiringly strives to secure, by having them copied in the abbeys that possess specimens. One of the most fascinating aspects of his correspondence is this hunt for manuscripts, for which he goes to so much trouble and expense—

---

[2] Ed. Olleris, p. 298, and J. Havet, *Lettres de Gerbert*, Paris, 1889.

promising a large reward at one time, and at another one of those celestial globes he knew how to build. By his efforts Terence, Virgil, Horace, Lucan, Statius, Persius, and Juvenal are saved—not for the delight of a bibliophile jealous of enlarging his treasure, or for the solitary enjoyment of a man of letters in the concealment of his study, but to enter into the mainstream of human thought, to be explained in public to the young, whom such a teacher knew how to inspire with the fire of his enthusiasm. His strong and delicate hands take up the vessel that St. Odilo had seen in a dream. But no serpents rise from it—it contains wisdom such as a Christian can and must profitably acquire. At the same time, this practical genius so well equipped for action introduces his students to the use of words; they discourse in Latin; the *conciones* in the manner of Sallust which Richerus uses, and which he places in the mouths of the characters of his history—to sum up a situation or explain the psychology of a decision or event—are surely due to Gerbert's teaching. The art of writing history will long retain this tradition—to the end of the classical period.

Even if Gerbert had done no more than teach the trivium, his name would be assured of a place in the history of the human mind. But he seems to have exercised an equally profound influence through his teaching of the quadrivium, mathematics—that is, arithmetic, music, geometry, and astronomy. In employing the abacus, he made use of a procedure that had been known since the fifth century, and was being practiced in Spain around 970. He had a craftsman build an abacus for him, and make a thousand "characters" of horn. It was a kind of counting machine, analogous to the abacus, with twenty-seven frames of three columns, a column for each series of figures, one for the units, another for the tens, and the last for the hundreds. Each number thus received a different value according to the column in which it was placed; calculation became much simpler and could be reduced to a mere movement of the hand, at least for dexterous users of the device. Though zero was unknown, and though fractions caused difficulty, it may be said that Gerbert's students, playing the abacus like an

17. Christ blessing Theophano and Otto II. Ivory. Cluny Musuem, Paris.
Tenth century. (*Photograph*: Archives Photographiques.)

instrument, were "juggling" with numbers. This explains Abbon's enthusiasm, and his bad verse. Some operations still were long and complicated. When Gerbert asked his Spanish correspondents for the treatise of Leo the Wise on multiplication and division, he did so to improve his method. He did the same in geometry. We possess a treatise in this science which bears his name, but in a handwriting postdating the manuscript. It has been assumed, with good reason, that it is the work of one of his students, perhaps lecture notes. The work mentions Pythagoras, Eratosthenes, the *Timaeus*, and the commentary of Chalcides. Gerbert, however, knew no Greek. How could he have known these authors? Through the Arabs? But Gerbert knew no Arabic. Most likely he knew them through Jewish translations into Latin. Pfister and Picavet reject this hypothesis, on the grounds that the journey to Cordova is a legend. In their day, hardly anything was known concerning intellectual life in Catalonia, and concerning Mozarabic culture. It was not necessary to go to Cordova, and to know Arabic, in order to be in touch with Jewish-Islamic science. The text relating to Leo the Wise is sufficient proof. This remark, however, in no way diminishes the value of their observations concerning the ancient sources of the Roman *agrimensores*.

Gerbert's greatest innovations are not those in geometry—nor in music. What Richerus has to tell us on the matter leads us to think that in this area Gerbert owed almost all he knew to Boethius' *De Musica*. It was not long after Gerbert's death that the monk Guido d'Arezzo advanced this art a decisive step by making the reading of tones and halftones simpler and more lucid. Still, Gerbert trained many a good musician, among them King Robert, who not only liked to sing in choir, but probably wrote music for hymns whose texts were composed by others, since they were know before his time; there is for instance O *constantia martyrum*, which Queen Constance in her innocence believed to have been written specially for her, because she had asked for it. But the most brilliant teaching Gerbert did was in astronomy and rhetoric. Here again, he drew without a doubt on Arab sources; his letter concerning the translation of the treatise *De Astrologia* is sufficient proof. Just as in teaching rhetoric, dialectic, and arithmetic, so here too Gerbert was not a pure theoretician, but demonstrated what he taught on the basis of tangible data. To this end he caused globes to be constructed of which Richerus speaks with enthusiastic delight: first a plain globe of wood, on which he marked the spots where the stars rise and set, also several armillary globes showing their course across the sky, and finally a hollow sphere equipped with several tubes, one of which made it possible to determine the poles, while the others, turning around the first, directed the eye and held it to a fixed point.[3] Gerbert's globes became famous. He was offered manuscripts in exchange—but patience was necessary, for he did not conceal the fact that building them required a great deal of time and labor.

Does this sketch afford us a complete impression of Gerbert's teaching, and of his scholarship? Surely not, since some of his students give evidence of interest in medicine and a certain knowledge of the subject. In the field of legal studies, he appears to have practiced canon law above all, but not to the point of recognizing the False Decretals which were submitted to him and which he accepted as authentic, though he discussed them with all the subtlety of his intellectual powers. Finally, he was a theologian, at least if we are to credit him with having written *De corpore et sanguine Domini*, whose author takes a position halfway between the partisans of the real presence and those who, like Rabanus Maurus, consider the bread and wine symbols of the Church, which is the body of Christ. But it is not in writings of this kind that we must look for the essence of Gerbert's genius, nor even in his brilliant dissertation on the rational, and the use of reason. His mathematical works are more important. But what defines his role and expresses his nature more than anything else is the way the insatiable curiosity of his intellect expressed itself in his life, and the way he shared it with a large part of the elite of his time.

---

[3] Richerus, *op. cit.*, Book III, Ch. L–LIII; see C. Pfister, *op. cit.*, p. 31, and F. Picavet, *op. cit.*, pp. 74ff.

A teacher realizes himself in his students as much as in his writings. In the front ranks of those whom Gerbert formed belongs Richerus, without whom the great professor of the school at Reims would not be as well known as he deserves. Gerbert's urging caused Richer to undertake the writing of the history of his times, whose four volumes cover the period from Charles the Fat and King Odo to the year 995. It is a priceless source for the years after 969, and especially for the revolution which raised Hugh Capet to the royal throne. Richerus was still alive in 998; after that date we have no information at all about him. He had a knowledge of medicine; in 991, he undertook the difficult journey from Reims to Chartres, to confer with the monk Hériband and consult certain medical manuscripts. Besides, Pfister rightly notes the space that Richerus devotes to the descriptions of the illnesses of which the characters of his *History* had died. Another of Gerbert's students, Fulbert, started with medicine; but he made a mark as the treasurer of St. Hilaire of Poitiers, and especially as bishop of Chartres—a mark not just in political life, where he became involved in more than one historic event of King Robert's day, but in the history of culture (under his episcopacy, Chartres attained great luster) and in the history of art, through the cathedral which he raised, which was destroyed by fire in 1194. Abbon of Fleury, we recall, came to Reims to acquire what knowledge he was still lacking. There were around Gerbert many others who would become noted in the monastic life or in the episcopacy—Ingon, abbot of St. Germain-des-Prés, of St. Pierre-le-Vif at Sens, and of Massay (founded in the year 1000); Gérard, bishop of Cambrai; Adalberon, bishop of Laon, who bore the same name as the archbishop of Reims and whom the people would some day name "the old traitor"; and finally Liétry, whom Robert would raise to archbishop at Sens in the year 1000. These were the youthful companions of the man destined to be King Robert—for Hugh Capet and Adelaide had entrusted their son's education to Gerbert. Under Gerbert's influence the young prince earned his titles—not the rather absurd nickname "the Pious" which our old historians bestowed on him in deference to his extremely stupid biographer Helgaud, but that other title given to him in certain charters under which we can read *regnante Roberto rege theosopho,* a phrase which may well be translated "the Christian philosopher."

We must cease regarding as totally barbarian a period in which we find the heir of the dukes of France among Gerbert's students, those brilliant young men whom he would later choose for offices of high authority in the Church. We must take account not only of the intrinsic value but of the breadth and impact of such teaching, which on the threshold of the year 1000 raises men of such talent for Capetian France. Gerbert's fame traveled beyond the French borders to Italy, and to Germany where it provoked the envy of Otric of Magdeburg. Otric was a scholar in the entourage of Otto I, and teacher of St. Adalbert, the Apostle of Bohemia. He thought that he could catch Gerbert out in the classification of the sciences, and sent one of his students to take notes in Gerbert's course to support his imputations. Armed with such proof, he informed Otto II of the disagreement, hoping, no doubt, to lower his rival's credit at the imperial court, where Gerbert had long been known and esteemed. The Emperor called Gerbert and Otric to Ravenna, to have them dispute before him; Richerus tells us the whole story of the dialectical contest from which Gerbert appears to have emerged undiminished in stature. The time was around Christmas of 980. Otric died the following year, on October 1, and thus was spared the bitter experience of having to see his opponent rise to still greater honors, not just in his academic career but in that astounding destiny which was to raise him to the papal throne. We tend to forget that there is something not quite honorable in the kind of espionage to which Otric had stooped, and only remember, as an interesting facet of the moral history of the period, this conference in Ravenna, where the Emperor himself presides over a debate on pure philosophy.[4]

[4] On the debate see F. Picavet, *op. cit.,* pp. 45–47.

18. (a) Seal of Robert the Pious (996–1031) (*Photograph*: Armand Colin.) (b) Seal of Otto III (996–1002) (*Photograph*: from *Bolletino d'Arte*, 1936.)

III

And now a new stage begins in Gerbert's life. He does not cease being a man of thought, but enters upon a life of action filled with difficulties, pitfalls, and trials. At the Ravenna conference he had faced nothing more than a disgruntled colleague. But from now on he will encounter tougher adversaries. It is his destiny to be one of those men who soar to their greatest heights only in battle. And he is prepared for battle, armed with every weapon for other struggles than mere intellectual rivalry. We should not wish to see him always untroubled.

At the end of 982 or the beginning of 983, he was made abbot of Bobbio, in Lombardy. Otto II, by calling him to rule St. Columbans' famous foundation, once more expressed his friendship for the scholar from Reims. Bobbio was remarkable for its possession, and perhaps still more remarkable for its ancient fame, for its library, and for the travels of these *peregrini Scotti* who, coming from Northumberland and Ireland, spread throughout the *scriptoria* of the monasteries many examples of the principles of book illumination in the form of their beautiful gospel manuscripts. We know that Bobbio's library was a rich source of delight for Gerbert. For its time, that library was encyclopedic: the works of the masters of profane antiquity stood side by side with those of the Church Fathers, the poets—Vergil, Horace, Ovid, Juvenal, Claudius—the orators and philosophers Cicero and Seneca, and even Lucretius who was then, and had long been, very little known. The sciences—astronomy, medicine—had their place along with literature. Later, after he had left Bobbio, Gerbert would often think of those riches—not with fruitless nostalgia, but for the purpose of spreading their beneficial influence. He wrote this charming and skillful letter to one of his faithful friends, the monk Rainard, in strictest confidence:

I urgently ask of you one thing only, which will not expose you to any risk or loss, and will tie even more closely the bonds of our friendship. You know the fervor with which I am everywhere looking for books; you know also how many copyists there are everywhere in the towns and countryside of Italy. To work, then, and without telling a soul have them copy for me the *Astronomy* of Manlius, the *Rhetoric* of Victorinus, Demosthenes' treatise on ophthalmia. I, my dear brother, undertake to keep inviolable silence about the favor you will do me. All the expenses you will have I shall repay with interest, at such a place as you will write me and at the time that you will set for me.[5]

But even while he was at Bobbio, he did not forget his own library at Reims: "Have the Pliny corrected," he wrote to Airard de Saint-Thierry, "have them send us Eugraphius, have copies made of the manuscripts that are at Orbais and at St. Basle. . . ." Nothing can quench this burning passion; once more we see what stuff this life is made of; whichever way we turn it, and even if we look only at a single facet of it, this life is dedicated to the spirit with an intensity such as was unknown even to the great cardinal-humanists of the Renaissance, men like Bessarion or Aeneas Silvius.

But the government of the abbey brought with it endless problems. Despite the luster of his name, he was received there as the Emperor's creature. Here as elsewhere, he knew how to inspire men with a deep devotion for him. Still, some remained partisans of his predecessor Petroald. The Italians distrusted Gerbert, and he was not fond of them. With a vigorous reticence that allows us only to guess his bitterness, he revised Vergil's verse: *Fruges, non viri*—fruits of the soil, yes; men, no. The vast properties of Bobbio were being raided by his vassals. The new abbot tried in vain to have his monastery's rights respected. Pierre, bishop of Pavia proposed to talk things over. Gerbert refused. "Go on robbing and stealing and arousing the forces of Italy against me. The moment is favorable; our master is busy making war . . ." [6] Where could he turn for support? Otto loved Gerbert well, but now more than ever his vast enterprises made it necessary for him to conciliate the Italians. When he dies on December 7, 983, the abbot of Bobbio

---

[5] J. Havet, *op. cit.*, Epist. 7, 8, 9; see F. Picavet, *op. cit.*, pp. 120ff.

[6] J. Havet, *op. cit.*, Epist. 5; see also F. Picavet, *op. cit.*, p. 53.

is left helpless; he cannot count on the Pope, the former bishop of
Pavia. He returns to France, leaving the abbey to Petroald without, however, surrendering his title. Some of his monks remained
attached to him and even came to visit him in Reims. Six years
later (989), he writes that Petroald is a "tyrant," in the strict
sense of the word—a usurper. Even so, after Gerbert has become
pope he will confirm Petroald in his position at Bobbio. For Gerbert is both a magnanimous man and a politician: he will not hold
a grudge over an old defeat.

The death of Otto II produced a complicated situation. The
son whom Theophano had borne him was then three years old.
Henry, duke of Bavaria, and Lothair, king of the Franks, aspired
to the guardianship—Henry in order to make himself master of
Germany, Lothair to carry out the Lorraine policies of the Carolingian kings. These vast lands, which included not only the Lorraine of the Moselle valley but also Lower Lorraine, the region
between Flanders and the Rhine, remained essentially the object
of their conflicting claims and, one might say, the basis of Carolingian irredentism. But the Empire held on to its rights in the
area, and those who were loyal to it persevered. Personal relations
within the structure of a feudal society are at times exceedingly
complex. Adalberon, archbishop of Reims and by that title a vassal of the king of the Franks, belonged to a family of Lorraine. He
had been educated at the abbey of Gorze in the diocese of Metz.
Furthermore, Bruno, the brother of Otto I and archbishop of
Cologne, had given him the countship of Hainaut. He was friendly
to the Empire, and his friend Gerbert, client of the House of
Saxony, shared his views. Both men endeavored to secure the neu-
trality of the duke of France in the contest brought about by the
minority of Otto III. They tried to dissuade Lothair from pursuing his plans. But Lothair was already marching on Verdun. At
this juncture, they conceived the idea of overthrowing the Carolingian dynasty, and to set in its place that powerful lordly family
which wielded almost royal authority both in their duchy and in
France. Gerbert's famous letter to an unknown correspondent

belongs here: "I am writing you an enigmatic letter in very few words: Lothair is king of France in name only; Hugh, it is true, is not king in name, but is in fact. If you seek his friendship and if you bind his son to the son of Caesar, the kings of France will no longer be your enemies." [7] Was this truly a service to the cause of France, this undertaking to replace a dynasty which, though headed by men of energy, had spent its strength, with a strong dynasty even at the price of abandoning—temporarily—the Lorraine policy? In any case, while the attitude of Adalberon, bishop of Reims and chancellor of the crown, may have been ambiguous, Gerbert's attitude was not. The death of Lothair on March 2 of 986, and of his son Louis V in May of 987, solved the problem. In June of this same year Hugh Capet, elected by the assembly of Senlis, was consecrated at Noyon. The following Christmas he had his son consecrated at Orléans. Thus Gerbert's political views were realized in history. Quite obviously Gerbert did not seek to aggrandize the Empire at the expense of France—on the contrary, he endowed France with new strength. Faithful both to his student at Reims and to the son of Otto II, Gerbert worked toward the equilibrium of the West.

These broad statesmanlike views, supported by events which assured their quick success, secured for Gerbert a moral authority that was not challenged. He had been the moving spirit of Adalberon's machinations; and whatever the archbishop of Reims and chancellor of France could not do or say in person, Gerbert had taken on himself. He had made and unmade kings. After he had become Hugh Capet's secretary, he could make his influence felt in the affairs of the monarchy. Adalberon's friendship and the prince's gratitude were his assurance that his fortune would hold. The archbishop thought of him as his successor, and even had so designated him. He dies on January 23, 989, and Gerbert is not named to succeed him. Instead, by a strange turn of fate, the successor was Arnulf, Lothair's bastard. We try in vain to understand

[7] J. Havet, *op. cit.*, Epist. 48.

the reason for this choice which was both politically unwise and hardly honorable on the part of Hugh Capet, who had been raised to the royal purple by Gerbert against Lothair's family. That family had not resigned itself to having lost its place. Charles, duke of Lorraine and Hugh Capet's former rival—and the legitimate heir besides—was Arnulf's uncle. Did the king of France hope that by making Arnulf an archbishop he could secure the nephew's support for himself against the uncle, and thus could split the Carolingians? If he did, he was quickly disabused. In 988, Duke Charles had carried Laon, the Carolingians' ancient acropolis and refuge of Lothair's widow Emma. He held it against royal troops through two sieges. One August night of 989, he takes possession of Reims by a surprise attack and with Arnulf's help. This stroke is the last tremor of a doomed race. What part did Gerbert have in the matter? After Arnulf had been made archbishop of Reims, Gerbert had remained close to him. He was still abbot of Bobbio, at least in name, and in fact the prelate's scholastic and secretary. He not only bowed to Charles but served the purpose of the two conspirators. He followed Terence's maxim, which is prudent rather than lofty: "If you cannot do what you will, will what you can do." This is in fact the low point of his life. He was in ill health, and confused. Hugh Capet's ingratitude and—we must say it—stupidity at this point may help us to understand, if not excuse, Gerbert's conduct. It has also been said that as the abbot and count of a great Italian abbey, to which Otto II had called him, he had feudal duties only to the Empire. It is painful for us to see him violate the great line of his political conception, so undeniably French and Capetian. We shall never take him for a cheap adventurer, avenging himself for a disappointment and tempting fate. This much is certain, the episode caused him great suffering, and he hastened to put an end to it as soon as possible. Strangely, Gerbert had become involved in the matter through a Carolingian prince, the son of one of Lothair's sisters; we have met him before—Bruno of Roucy, bishop of Langres.

Anyway, Gerbert made his peace, and the king showed understanding.

In 991, the adventure of the Lorraine pretender is ended. Laon
falls on the night of Palm Sunday; it is surrendered by its bishop,
Adalberon or Ascelin, who earlier had bound himself with the
most sacred vows to the cause of the two Carolingians, and who
betrays Arnulf as Arnulf had betrayed Hugh Capet. The duke and
the archbishop are confined at Orléans; the prelate then is sum-
moned before a council convened at St. Basle-de-Verzy on June
17 and 18. Arnulf was condemned for his felony, stripped of his
dignities, and returned to jail. But did a national council have the
right to make such a decision without the consent of the Holy See?
We know what the bishops thought of the Sovereign Pontiff.
Abbon of Fleury, spokesman of the monks against the bishops,
upheld the rights of the Pope and based himself on the False
Decretals. Gerbert opposed them; it was Gerbert who was elected
archbishop.

IV

The error of hagiographers is to think that in a great life all
things are great. In human terms, the misery and the pettiness
with which Gerbert now struggles do not reduce his stature. But
it is a sad spectacle to see the archbishop of Reims and chancellor
of France defending his title against the papacy and the King of
France himself. He despised these altercations which turned him
away from higher concerns. He tells us that he would much rather
have fought against men at arms. Yet he entered these battles,
which are so unprofitable to the mind, with all the firmness, all
the sternness that are characteristic of him, and with all his powers
of dialectic. The report of St. Basle-de-Verzy alone impresses upon
us the extent and subtlety of those powers! [8] Was this report written from stenographic notes, as Julien Havet believes? It is not
impossible that Gerbert learned the skill of shorthand in Italy,

[8] See A. Olleris, Œuvres de Gerbert, p. 213; on the Council of St. Basle, see E.
Amann et A. Dumas, Histoire de l'Église, Vol. 7, Paris, 1948, pp. 70–73.

where it was in use among the notaries. But I find it difficult to believe that the debates of the Council did in fact possess such an elegant, unified structure. The speech of the bishop of Orléans, for instance, whose basic content is beyond a doubt correct, is a beautiful address altogether worthy of Gerbert's own pen. This beauty, and this liveliness of form do not, incidentally, detract in any way from the historical authenticity of such a document edited by a witness of this caliber.

At all events, the Pope's legate had witnessed how his master had been treated with a violence that further heightened the indignation of John XV, who was already outraged at seeing his rights abused. He made attempts to secure the intervention of the prelates of Germany and Lorraine; at Aix-la-Chapelle and at Ingelsheim, he was successful in obtaining a condemnation of the decisions of St. Basle-de-Verzy. Accordingly, he excommunicates Gerbert. But the Council of Chelles, presided over by young King Robert, decides that one may not obey the Pope when the Pope is not just. At this point, the splendid arrangement of the Council of Mouzon comes into play. The Pope is in need of a few French bishops and above all of a German majority that does not stand in awe of the king of France. Mouzon, a border town, depended on Reims ecclesiastically, while politically it depended on Lorraine. Hugh Capet forbade his bishops to take part in the Council there. Gerbert went alone (995), and delivered an address whose text is disputed.[9] But his efforts yielded no precise results. The assembly disbanded, deciding that another council be convened, to be held at Rome this time. It never met.

It does not seem that Gerbert's patience had been exhausted by these delays and detours of a political craftiness that did not shock the French bishops. But when young Otto III was going to Rome to receive the imperial crown, the archbishop of Reims decided to accompany him and plead his cause in person before the Pope (997). This undertaking is not only in the grand manner

[9] On the Council of Mouzon, see E. Amann and A. Dumas, *op. cit.*, pp. 73–74; the texts are in Richerus, *Historiarum libri IV*, Book IV, Ch. CI–CIV.

—it is exceedingly clever, because the occasion of the coronation and Otto's friendship seem made to further Gerbert's interests. The intervening events have changed his luck, and changed it for the better. John XV dies. He is replaced by a relative of Otto III, Gregory V. But luck turns once again: Hugh Capet's death deprives Gerbert of a master who had supported him constantly since their reconciliation.

Hugh Capet is succeeded by Robert, Gerbert's former pupil. Here is another card which may be played handsomely. Did not Robert preside over the Council of Chelles? Does he not know, as well as did his father, the full weight which Gerbert's influence, his genius, his political skill have had—just ten years ago—in changing the destiny of the House of Capet? Robert, however, loved Bertha, his kinswoman. He had to have the Pope's agreement to a union which risked condemnation by the Church, and was in fact so condemned; Richerus tells us that Gerbert candidly opposed the marriage. Besides, Robert was friendly toward Abbon who, we recall, took his stand at St. Basle-de-Verzy against Gerbert for many reasons; some of them were canonical and extremely weak, since they rested upon false texts, others were political and drew their support from the opposition between monks and bishops; still others, finally, stemmed from the surliness of his person. Abbon was the man who at the Pope's request advised Robert to release Arnulf. It was a superb joke played on the bishops of St. Basle-de-Verzy by an embittered and skillful monk (November 997).

Gerbert heard of it in Germany, where he had gone after a short journey to France. Reims was no longer of concern to him even now. His enemies there were inciting the soldiery and clerics against him. This beautiful world, which he had built and borne up with his own hands for ten long years, now relapsed into politics and barbarism. At the court of an emperor seventeen years of age and filled with enthusiasm for study and lofty ideas, an Emperor whose forebears had been Gerbert's unfailing friends and benefactors, Gerbert felt that he had arrived at the true vocation

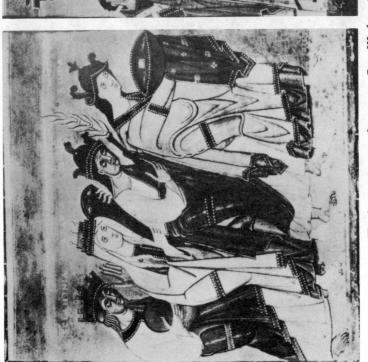

19. The four nations pay homage to Otto III, from "Otto III's Gospel." Latin manuscript 4453, Munich Library. Around 1000. (*Photograph:* Stoedtner.)

of his intellect; and his powerful life of the mind, his humanist's passion for the greatness of ancient Rome, together with his devotion to the House of Saxony, were to inspire him with his supremely daring conception of European stability. Otto asked Gerbert to educate him. As early as the end of 997, in return for the gift of Boethius' *Arithmetic*—a handsome copy on which Gerbert had inscribed three poems—Otto wrote him a letter full of allusions, closing with a short rhythmic, rhymed poem, Otto's first poetic composition. He called on Gerbert to come to his assistance in completing his neglected education so that he might strip off his Saxon boorishness by awakening his natural Greek sensibility. He refers with pride to Greece, his mother's native land, and with regret to his Saxon rusticity: "*Volumus vos Saxonicam rusticitatem abhorrere, sed grecsicam nostram subtilitatem ad id studii magis vos provocare.*" [10]

This splendid and sensitive prince bestowed on Gerbert the domain of Sasbach in Alsatia as a gift. He took him along to Italy, where troubles had erupted in Rome. There, they learned that Arnulf had been released; his reinstatement as archbishop of Reims was now a certainty. Otto, by making Gerbert archbishop of Ravenna, nobly put an end to a hopeless situation. The Pope had no alternative but to confirm a choice which set Reims definitively free. In April 998, the new archbishop of Ravenna assumed his see.

We must pause here to consider this moment in Gerbert's life, when he can tell himself that his troubles had ended in the most honorable manner, in this city where the memories of the last emperors and the last traces of the majesty of Rome fused with the vestiges of another lofty idea, Justinian's attempt to restore the unity of the Empire to the Mediterranean. Ravenna was a better place than Aix-la-Chapelle, the distant capital of the North—a better place even than Rome, torn by the strife of factions—for the most accomplished mind of the tenth century to cherish his

---

[10] "Strip me of my Saxon boorishness, develop what I have in me of my Greek origin. . . ." J. Havet, *op. cit.*, Epis. 186–187; see also F. Picavet, *op. cit.*, p. 105.

dream, not of continuing the glorious past perhaps, but at least of the possibility to revive it. Everything there was inviting him—a century-old tradition, the very monuments of the city, Maximianus' ivory chair embellished with Hellenistic carvings on which Gerbert was now seated in his turn. There still persisted in Ravenna a humanism which was to take on new life in the form of a heresy, if we are to accept the word of Glaber (who no doubt distorts the facts with his Cluniac prejudices). Vilgard, in a dream, saw Vergil, Horace, and Juvenal resuscitated by the Devil. They expressed thanks to their disciple for the care with which he sought their glory, and promised him that he would share in it. From then on Vilgard preached the ancient poets like a new gospel. Glaber tells us that the heresiarch's sectarians were numerous in Italy, and that they had to be destroyed with fire and sword. Vilgard of Ravenna is no more than an episode—both painful and encouraging—in the long history of this devotion to a vanished past, a devotion of which Gerbert himself had shown so many striking signs in Reims and elsewhere.

We do not know much, really, about the year Gerbert spent at Ravenna, beyond the fact that he brought to his administration those principles of order and regularity which, years earlier, he had vainly attempted to impose upon the Italian lawlessness of Bobbio. He was still abbot of Bobbio even now. He saw to it that the squandered possessions were restored to the monastery, and a limit put on long-term leases. He called together the bishops of his archdiocese to institute measures concerning the discipline of the clergy. Having himself come from a country where that virtue was practiced, the abbot of Hersfeld explains, he tried to spread its blessings elsewhere. We must not imagine Gerbert purely as an intellectual, content to have found a last asylum, deep studies, and fine books. Wherever he is called, he always does much more than merely carry out the duties of his post; he has a liking and a gift for action to the point of open conflict. This combination of a lofty mind with the will for constructive work is surely the key

20. Emperor Otto III. Relief from well, St. Bartolomeo all'Isola, Rome. Eleventh Century (?). (*Photograph:* Dr. Hilde Bauer, from *Jahrbuch der preussischen Kunstsammlungen,* 1936.)

to his destiny; it is for us the conclusive explanation of the Pope of the year 1000.

When Gregory V died in February 999, the archbishop of Ravenna was called to be his successor. Monk at Aurillac, student and then scholastic at Reims, Adalberon's friend, Queen Emma's secretary, Hugh Capet's secretary, abbot of Bobbio, archbishop of Reims, disputed by the Pope, abandoned by the King, a young Emperor's counsellor, and finally raised by that Emperor to one of Italy's highest honors—can we find in all history a richer life, a better preparation even in adversity for the exercise of a sovereign power? He knows the diversity of peoples—Aquitaine, Spain, northern France, Italy, Germany. His scholarship embraces the entire knowledge of his time. He has made and unmade kings. He has dreamed of conciliating France and Germany by a dynastic revolution. He is about to attempt an even grander design when he tries to restore the Empire of Constantine. The master who offers him the unique opportunity is a young prince born to understand Gerbert, and steeped in Gerbert's thought. At that time, the Emperor held the power to bestow the tiara. When he placed it on Gerbert's head, he did not make him his "creature." He did not even gain for himself a clever ally in pursuing the Italian politics of the Ottonians. The bonds that unite the youth and the mature man are of different kinds. They answer to a higher vow which is in part illuminated by the fine letter from which we have just quoted. Rome was the place where the two tried to carry out that vow. Rome is the scene to which we must now turn, until that sorrowful evening in the year 1002 when the death of the young Caesar put an end to the dream of universal empire.

FOUR

The Universal Empire

ON Pentecost Sunday of the year 1000, young Emperor Otto III,[1] recently crowned in Rome, is standing in the old palace chapel of Aix, gazing at the remains of Charlemagne, whose forgotten grave had been found at his command. Contrary to the legend, the founder of the Empire is not seated on a throne, scepter and globe in hand. He lies in an antique sarcophagus, around his neck a cross of gold. This solemn meeting adds to the greatness of the times. It takes its place in the history of the idea of Empire, not as a strange episode but as an event charged with significance. Otto III does not aspire to hold an empty title but to renew a tradition of centuries, to take Charlemagne as his exemplar, and to restore the universal empire, *imperium mundi*. His father and his grandfather had come to the Eternal City before him to receive the crown and the imperial dignity. But those chieftains of Germanic troops camped on the Monte Mario looked upon the Empire as family property, an addition to the power of Germany. They never took the Empire's full measure. They often found it a burden

[1] For the entire present chapter on Otto III, see A. Fliche, *L'Europe occidentale de 838 à 1125*, Paris, 1930, pp. 218ff.; M. Ter Braak, *Kaiser Otto III, Ideal und Praxis im frühen Mittelalter*, Amsterdam, 1928; E. P. Schramm, *Kaiser, Rom und Renovatio* (*Studien der Bibliotek Warburg*, Vol. XVII), Berlin, 1929, 2 vols.

when they became involved in the fury of the wars of Italy. But the son of the Greek Empress, the pupil of Gerbert, cherished a larger vision: to the imperial title which adorned the Saxon Caesars, he would lend the twofold authority of holiness—by a close union with the Church in heart and mind—and of Romanity, by spreading the Roman spirit throughout the Roman domain. Had not Charlemagne been a saint? This holy Emperor, this new Constantine, was in the thoughts and prayers of Otto III as he stood there on that Pentecost day before the rediscovered bones.

The dethronement and death of Charles the Fat mark the end of the Carolingian Empire (888). The Empire falls apart; each of the kingdoms rising from its ruins after terrible disorders achieves its independent political life. Its title still survives for a time; it is assumed in turn by the princes of the House of Spoleto, by Arnulf, King of Germany, a Carolingian by blood but illegitimate, and by Louis and Berenger, kings of Italy. The fall of the Empire is soon followed by the fall of the imperial dignity which had lived on weakly after the political reality had disappeared. Neither Germany nor Italy nor France, where the Carolingian line continues, attempts to resurrect it. But while it has been erased from public life, it has not been erased from the memory of the nations. At the close of the ninth century Lambert of Spoleto had laid down the doctrine in his book *Libellus de imperatoria potestate*.[2] In the middle of the next century, Adso of Montiérender, addressing himself to Gerberga queen of France, asserts that the world cannot perish as long as there are Frankish kings, because the imperial dignity resides in them. It is a remarkable text, whose importance we have stressed before, and whose interest lies not only in showing the endurance of the imperial idea, but also in connecting it so closely with the Frankish monarchy and the Carolingian family. At the same time the legend of Charlemagne began to spring up, in its primitive and popular expressions; Benedict of Mont-Soracte rendered the oldest version of an episode famous in this legend,

[2] On this text, see A. Lapotre, *L'Europe et le Saint-Siège à l'époque carolingienne*, Paris, 1895, Vol. I, pp. 192 ff.

the journey to Jerusalem. Rome remained deeply steeped in this nostalgia. As the city of coronations and the tomb of the Apostles, she was the goal of countless pilgrimages: Flodoard documents it for the years 931 to 940. The imperial idea and the idea of Rome, it could be said, never become separated. The memory and the promise they contain offer consolation amid the vast sorrows of the world.

Thus a tradition, a legend, a nostalgia were preparing the way for the Empire's return. It still surprises us that the return did not take place in France, this ancient Carolingian soil where vigorous Carolingians still ruled, this country of the Franks whose kings, Adso asserted, carried the imperial dignity within them. It is hard to believe that his remark is the appeal, the allusion of an isolated man of letters. Perhaps the French kings of that time had more courage than imagination. Their energies were absorbed by the dynastic struggles which came to an end with the revolution of 987 in which the Capetians triumphed. Italy herself was strife-torn and in no position to lay claim to the Empire. Meanwhile the House of Saxony was on the ascendancy in Germany. On the battlefield of Riade, where Duke Henry I had crushed the Hungarians, his soldiers had acclaimed him, shouting, "Long live the Emperor!" The cry presages the destiny that awaits his son Otto I, crowned king in 936. Did men look forward then to a restoration of the imperial office? We know that the ceremonial of 936 is Frank, and that the bishop of Mainz, when he presents the sword, speaks these words: "Receive this sword with which you will drive off all enemies of Christ, barbarians and bad Christians, and by which God gives you power over the entire Empire of the Franks—*auctoritate divina tibi tradita omnipotestate totius imperii Francorum.*" [3] The phrase is purely formulary, since Roman France is excluded; but its political meaning, affirming the *imperium*, is incontestable. The Frankish genealogy with which the Saxons are endowed has the same significance. It makes them

---

[3] Widukind, *Rerum gestarum saxonicarum libri*, Book II, Ch. 1, 2; see also R. Koepke and F. Duemmler, *Kaiser Otto der Grosse*, Leipzig, 1876, pp. 37ff.

legitimate; it connects them not only with Charlemagne but with the great Merovingians. Such acclamations of armies, ceremonial formularies, and pseudo-genealogies are items of interest in the history of the idea of *imperium*, but they would not have been enough to found the Empire. Otto came closer to it through his kingship of Italy. But when he seizes the crown (962), he does so on the strength of his armed might, after impressive and repeated victories over the barbarians—almost under the same circumstances as Charlemagne, to whom he is compared enthusiastically by the chroniclers of his day.

Thus the idea has become a fact; it has left the realm of mere speculation and entered into historical reality. The clerics who were dreaming of the Empire in the hands of a leader, not of weak heirs, had had time to think on the matter; the first two Saxons who had held the office had barely had the time to maintain and preserve it. Otto I and Otto II did not lack sensitivity to excellence in men or to great cultural concerns, as their relationship with Gerbert proves. But their true role was to make war. The whole drama of medieval Germany is written in bold strokes, like a mighty sketch, in the history of the first two Saxon emperors; and the third, Otto III, will be crushed by the burden. France at that same period is not without her own considerable problems, but they are problems of an altogether different order. She is no longer open to barbarian invasions except in the south, but there her defense rests on the province of Barcelona and the Christian kingdoms of the peninsula; and the Norman raids are no longer so frequent and intense. The action of Charles the Simple has been a success. The battle now is fought within, between the monarchy and its enemies. In Germany, too, the national duchies may at any moment rise up against the sovereign if his power falters or he is taken up with wars abroad; but Germany has, besides, retained this role of serving as a buffer zone "against the enemies of Christ, barbarians and bad Christians," which the Gaul of Clovis and the Gaul of Charlemagne had performed for so long. Germany confronts the barbarians of the north, the east, and the southeast, the

Vikings, the Wends, the Obotrites, the Poles, the Hungarians, the Slavs of Bohemia. Finally, in the south of Italy and in Sicily, the Empire stands face to face with Islam. In other parts of the peninsula, other threats were menacing the Empire—the turbid backwaters of a feudal structure forever ready to burst into disorder, the instability of a population whose only constancy was its enduring hostility toward the man from the north, the deep corruption of the papacy, the turbulence of the Roman barons, by long tradition holders of sacerdotal offices; farther south, the Lombard princes of Apulia, and finally the Greek *strategoi* who represent the authority of Byzantium in the southernmost parts of the peninsula. A whole world full of strife, discord, revolts, intrigue, a human *fauna* of feudal wildcats, simoniacal bishops, highway robbers with noble names, entrenched in the tombs of the Via Appia or in the little lacustrine castles of Upper Italy, that horrible pandemonium of crime which Hugo describes in Ratbert. Dethroned princes have their eyes plucked out, popes are strangled in the moats of Castel Sant' Angelo, district leaders are hanged, and Benedict of Mont-Soracte weeps tears over Italy's deep misery. To subject, to appease this tragic she-wolf would have required not only Otto's hard-fisted genius but his continuous presence. The Empire is forever in jeopardy. How often did the sentries of the Brenner Pass see his soldiers going and returning! No sooner have they gained a little respite in Italy than they must rush to Stargard or to Havelberg which are attacked, taken, by the Slavs. Matters are even worse if the Empire suffers a defeat somewhere: furious war breaks out again somewhere else. One of the facts that all of Otto's historians stress is that he never had the time to consolidate his position anywhere. His life is spent in maintaining, by sheer force, an equilibrium on the verge of collapse.

What will become of this vast fragile structure under a master such as Otto II, short, fat, sensuous, infatuated with himself and untouched by any higher insights? After the disastrous battle of Cape Colon, where he barely made his escape from the Arabs and where the bishop of Augsburg and the abbot of Fulda died in battle, the Dane invades Germany, the Slav puts Hamburg to the torch. All Europe rises in revolt. The Christians of most recent standing in the north give way before the barbarians, and those of central Europe are threatening to slip from their German allegiance and become nationals. But Otto II persists in being concerned with the affairs of Italy, with his negotiations with the bishops of Apulia and Calabria. At the assembly in Verona, men plead with him, admonish him. St. Majolus, abbot of Cluny, shows him how immense is the danger, how imminent the disaster, He does not listen, plans the conquest of Sicily, and descends upon the Abruzzi. This is the moment when Gerbert, abbot of Bobbio, writes that bitter letter to Peter, bishop of Pavia. While the Emperor is abroad, men take advantage of his absence. The situation can be put in a few words: the master of the Empire is always busy elsewhere. At last, in December 983, he dies. The frontiers of northern Germany are wide open. The heir to the throne is three years old.

It is a remarkable fact that those explosive events which normally accompany a regency did not occur. Germany doubtless sensed the danger; doubtless her loyalty to the House of Saxony had not weakened. But the skill of Theophano did the rest. In the first part of her life she catches our eye mostly by her brilliant appearance, her beauty, her splendor, her sophistication. As the daughter of Romanus II, she had grown up among the splendor and intrigue of the court of Byzantium. As the wife of Otto II, she had more than once accompanied the Emperor on his Italian campaigns. Now she is alone, at the age of twenty-seven, still radiant against that dark background, but unpopular because of certain unwise words she had let slip after the disaster of Cape Colon. She restores her moral authority in Germany and effects a reconciliation; at the same time, she reconciles the Italians and the Greeks by abandoning the conquest of Sicily and the struggle against Islam. Theophano had understood the warnings uttered at Verona. Even better, on the death of Boniface VII, she allows the Romans to elect a pope of their own choice, John XV. Finally, in order to avert the Slavic peril, she pits Poland against Bohemia and in the end reconciles the two. She had grasped the truth that if she was to save the Empire she must be queen of Germany rather than Empress of the West. At her exceedingly premature death (991) the aged Adelaide, her mother-in-law, widow of Otto I, follows the same policies and wages the war against the Wends. Both women, one Greek and the other Italian, had shown a better understanding of the immediate interests of Germany, and of the paradox of an Empire reeling from one crisis to another, than had the Saxon Otto II. When Otto III reaches majority (996), after having made war in the north since he was twelve—what will he choose? In which direction do his nature, his origins, his education incline him? What are the secret inclinations that inspire his thoughts, there before the remains of Charlemagne, in Aix-la-Chapelle, on Pentecost day of the year 1000?

II

The adolescent on whose shoulders rests the terrible burden of the Empire is a romantic hero, a political idealist, and a saint all in one. He has dreamed by turns of being Emperor of the world, and of the total abandonment of all worldly vanities. By turns, he treats the Romans to the spectacle of his holy majesty in theocratic ceremonies, and seeks complete solitude in a hut built of mud and rushes. At one time, he joins St. Adalbert and St. Nil in their most burning ecstasies of faith; at another time, he listens to the counsel of the old Gerbert, great in mind and great perhaps in intrigue, an honest man full of wise tricks, friend of the devil and prince of humanists. Was there ever a man whose nature was more readily provoked to the extremes of ambition and revulsion than he, still so young, whose days, which were already numbered, would leave no room for the balance and compromises of experience? His very disenchantment is a burning flame, and the world's reality is to him a living dream. He had the good fortune to die before his passions died, the noblest passions inspiring any man of his time—to disappear at the moment when his grand illusions were perhaps slipping away from him. In order that the spectrum of mankind be complete, history must at intervals show us such figures as he; then history reaches the supreme heights of fiction.

How are we to explain that this strange man had sprung from the seed of Otto the Great, that the rugged realist should have this heroic dreamer for a grandson? Of course, we have already observed a certain lack of good sense in Otto II, who at the time of greatest peril set his heart on the vain adventure of a crusade.

The explanation that is offered first, and rightly so, is the Greek blood flowing in the son's veins. Otto III has inherited its secret drive, but not its wisdom. It is a certainty that he was nursed on tales about the greatness of imperial Byzantine, and grew up surrounded by the cult of the past. Philagathus of Rossano taught him his mother tongue; Bernward, the famous abbot of Hildesheim, probably gave him a more solid education; and finally, we have seen the affection he felt for the old friend of the family, Gerbert. In the letter to Gerbert in which he thanked him for the gift of Boethius' *Arithmetic*,[4] we find him talking of his Saxon boorishness for which he blushes, and of that spark of Greek genius which needs to be rekindled. Gerbert could not fail to draw his conclusions from this effusive confession. In the happy formulation Gerbert uses, with the elegant precision of the great stylist —*genere graecus, imperio Romanus*, Greek by race, Roman by the Empire—we may discern the future of a grander, more brilliant, and in human terms more legitimate idea of empire than the Empire of the Saxons.

But in our view Otto's "Greekness," authentic as it is, also and perhaps first of all means a pride, a dedication of his spirit. Did it perhaps set free, as by a shock, those profoundly Germanic aspirations which we notice already in his father, though then much weaker? The eternal fascination that Italy has for the men from the north, the artificial nature of this world Empire, the cere-

---

[4] J. Havet, *op. cit.*, Epist. 186; F. Picavet, *op. cit.*, p. 105. This letter is discussed above. On the terms of the *Libellus de rationali et ratione uti* of Gerbert (dedicated to Otto), see A. Olleris, *op. cit.*, p. 298 and J. Havet, *op. cit.*, p. 236.

monies, the ostentatious pomp, everything, even this ancestor dug up from the grave, even this intensity of study, the deference of the *famulus* for his old Doctor Faustus from Aquitaine—all these are character traits in Otto III that are part of the genius of Germany. If Gerbert is a forerunner of Renaissance humanism, the young Emperor is a forerunner of German Romanticism. His story could have been put on stage, with astonishing harmony of motives, if not by Goethe then at least by one of the *Sturm und Drang* dramatists—not so much because of its violent episodes as because of the strangeness of its hero, and the fatality that rushes him toward his end. Even within the narrowest time span, history does perhaps encompass every variety of human type, and the whole repertory of situations. But this life, which was cut short so soon, offers only suggestions, of the sort of which the careers of Barbarossa and of Frederick II surely provided fuller elaboration.

In 996, Otto leaves for Italy to receive the imperial crown. The Slavs are contained, Italy seems assured. But as he clears the Alps, Verona revolts, and the city must be appeased. In Pavia comes news of the death of John XV; and Otto, from Ravenna, causes the election of his cousin and chaplain Benno, who takes the name of Gregory V. Gregory is a German, and a man of fierce energy—two reasons why he is despised in Rome. This first gesture, which departs equally from the wisdom of Theophano and the complacent softness of John XV, inevitably arouses fury. Once again that breed of rabble chiefs rises up who look upon the papacy as their private property, and oppose the resistance of feudal Rome to the German Empire. Gregory V, driven from Rome, retreats to Lombardy, awaiting the Emperor's intervention. Crescenzi, son of the rebel of 974, has Philagathus elected; Philagathus has just returned from Constantinople, where he had gone to seek the hand of an imperial princess for Otto III. This is neither the first nor the last of those uprisings that stain the city of the Caesars with blood spilled in fierce street fighting. Later on, the popular imagination will interpret them as national move-

ments, a kind of tribune's call, a call for freedom! Was that imagination as wholly wrong as it is claimed? True, the Latin barons
meant above all to preserve their exorbitant privileges, but the feelings that burst to the surface in the Verona revolt and later, during
the melancholy return of Otto's corpse to Germany, are proof
of something deeper and more meaningful. Crescenzi is neither
a hero nor a saint. The Rome of the year 1000 is not the Rome of
the Gracchi. But in the setting of the ruins of the Republic and
the Empire, those savage feudal lords acquire a measure of greatness.

By and large, that Rome was not very different from the city
which the brilliant visionary Piranese would show us later, in the
pale light of his etchings, which clashes with dark shadows. We
must forget the buildings of the Renaissance, and the Baroque;
what remains are the monuments of antiquity, long since corroded
by the weather, crumbling into ruins, covered with weeds and
brambles, charred with the fires of the great invasions, pierced at
every juncture by the thieves who removed their copper braces.
Just as in the days of our architect-engraver, patchwork repair
made it possible for men to inhabit them still, so now men lived
in Rome's caverns from which they sallied forth to do their evil
deeds. Crenellated, barricaded, bristling with wooden entangle-
ments, the tombs and temples boasted of their powerful solid
masonary which no battering ram could shake. The narrow streets
were made for ambuscades and traps. Did Rome have then, perhaps, as the Tuscan towns later, those narrow, square castle keeps
that rise up in mutual rivalry? Rome's ruins, especially, had turned
into fortresses. They have always been haunted by a strange population. Those little people who until quite recently lived in the
Theater of Marcellus are the successors of Crescenzi's men at
arms. There were other redoubts on the hills of Tusculum, peo-
pled by his brothers in rebellion. But for an understanding we must
go to Piranese's Rome with its powerful and melancholy *chiaro-
scuro*. In the Castel Sant' Angelo, he withstood a siege by imperial
troops that lasted two months. Only when he comes to the

Prisons, the outraged imagination of our artist begins to give us hints of the horrible torment inflicted on rebels, of popes strangled or starved to death. An Anchorite nearly a hundred years old, St. Nil, went to Otto to plead for Philagathus: Rome had been taken (February 998), the pope of the revolution was being paraded through the streets of his town riding on an ass. And Crescenzi's corpse was hoisted on the gallows of Monte Mario.

Could it have been these horrible events, or the exhortations of St. Nil, that worked that mystical crisis in Otto which drove him to take the roads that very year, in the midst of winter and on foot, to the oratory of Monte Gargano? He seems never to have made a separation between his function as an Emperor and his most austere duties as a Christian. The misery and scandal of the Church were his own fault. He sought a cure not just by means of probity in the pontifical administration; he wanted to redeem the fault in his own person. That moment, which appears to us as a crisis, is surely no more than the peak of a continual condition. There was indeed no split, his twofold duty accompanied Otto everywhere; neither St. Nil's hermitage at Serperi, nor the sanctuary of St. Michael on Monte Gargano kept him from knowing of the difficulties of Monte Cassino, or the unrest at Capua and Naples which he was trying to appease. But an unexpected turn of events places the papacy once more in jeopardy. Gregory V dies on February 18, 999. The Emperor raises Gerbert to the pontifical throne. It is as though history wiped the slate clean at this moment, to make room for new foundations—or new visions. The old German forces disappear. Death takes not only Gregory V but also the Emperor's grandmother Adelaide, and his aunt Mathilda to whom Otto had lately entrusted Germany during his absence—the "three pillars of Christendom." The death of his close and much loved relatives recalls the Emperor to Germany at the beginning of the year 1000. During his stay there, which lasts for six months, he causes the exhumation of Charlemagne. He then returns to Rome in the early autumn, intending to establish himself there. He has made his choice between the ancient capital of the Carolingians and the Eternal City. Only in Rome can the universal monarchy be founded. From Rome, it can cast its radiance throughout the Christian world.

III

These vast designs lack firm outlines in a true sense, as may well have been noted. But in this fact lies their interest and their originality. What is at stake is not the construction of a compact Empire, clearly defined by the territories that are its properties, or by sharply drawn frontiers. Nor is the issue that of treating the conversion of the barbarians as an instrument of Germanization; rather, the new Christian nations are to be free to live and grow within the framework of the Empire. The tie that is to bind them to the Empire is spiritual rather than feudal. Basically this conception is no more Constantinian than it is Carolingian. It rests upon the close union between emperor and pope. It is, if you will, one aspect of what is called Caesaropapism, but not in the sense of the exploitation of a papal vassal by the German kings. Gerbert joins the imperial power and his own into a single sovereignty that does not separate spiritual and temporal matters. Here lies the explanation, as Julien Havet has clearly shown, of the Pope's curious answer to the letter addressed to him by Robert the Pious, complaining about one of the saddest prelates of the times, the famous bishop of Laon, Adalberon, also called Ascelin. The complaint is said to have come to the hands of both the Emperor and the Pope: *Apostolicis et imperialibus oblata est manibus.*[5] What does the Emperor have to do with this matter of ecclesiastical discipline? The differences that may arise between the French episcopacy and King Robert are wholly within the Pope's competence, since the king is in no way, in no respect, a vassal of the Empire; France is not one of the kingdoms of which the Empire is com-

[5] See also Ph. Jaffe-G. Wattenbach, *Re gesta pontificum romanorum*, new edition, 1885–1888, No. 3914. On Gerbert's policies in this regard, see E. Amann and A. Dumas, *Histoire de l'Église*, Vol. 7, *L'Église au pouvoir des laïques*, with references, Paris, 1948.

posed—these are Germany, Lorraine, and Italy. But Gerbert and Otto look forward, beyond the political realities of the day, toward a state of the world when the joint will of pope and Emperor will arbitrate and govern all of Christendom. We have other "encroachments" on the king's authority: the count of Barcelona, a vassal of France, and the archbishop of Vich, between whom certain rights are at issue, are called, not before the king but before Otto III. We are not entirely justified in concluding that the first French pope followed an anti-French policy, because, as we shall see, his policies toward the newly converted nations could equally well be called anti-German. In fact, his policies serve the imperial idea first of all, and this idea transcends the perspectives of a Germanic imperialism.

The first pioneers of Christianity among the Slavs along the borders of the Empire had worked for the expansion of Germany as well. This was the course followed by such men as the famous Pilgrim of Passau. The bishopric of Prague, established in 975 or 976, was under the archbishops of Mainz. When Otto III and Gerbert installed the brother of Duke Boleslav as bishop of Prague, after a monk from Corvey had been nominated, they accepted the risk that a national Church might grow up in Bohemia. They did the same in Poland, where the bishopric of Posen, originally under Magdeburg, and those of Kolberg, Cracow, and Breslau, were jointly placed under the newly established archbishopric of Gnesen, site of St. Adalbert's tomb. This event took place in the early months of the year 1000, when Otto III had come to pray at St. Adalbert's tomb. Even more telling is the Hungarian example. In 995, Duke Geysa had been promised an illustrious match for his son—the promised bride was Gisela, daughter of Bavaria—on condition that he would convert to Christianity and help in the conversion of his people. Between 971 and 991, the bishop of Passau had already been successful in restoring his diocese, and even in introducing Germanism and Christianity into the Leitha region. But in the year 1000, Duke Waik, son of Geysa, receives the crown of gold that makes him king, together with a bull of enthronement from Sylvester II, who attaches the new kingdom to the Holy See as an apostolic monarchy. The bull has been contested, but the fact is incontestable: from now on there exists one more hereditary royalty, with a Church ruled by a metropolite. Waik adopts the name of Stephen—and under this name, the son of a brigand leader will become a saint of the Church. Whether Hungary has become a German colony or not is beside the point. The Empire has created a buffer zone, and turned back the barbarians. Just like the Normans whom Charles the Simple established permanently on French soil, so the Hungarians retain their ancient instincts. We shall soon see them in action, in the disorders that follow upon the death of Stephen (1042); but all the same they are henceforth a part of Europe's body.

We need not fear to overstress the originality of this structure which, rather than incorporate into the German kingdom provinces or feudatory states, added new kingdoms to the three that made up the Empire, and which, while it respected the idea of the national, superimposed on it a higher idea, in harmony with the very essence of Christianity, something that we might call the super-nation. The two terms—the apostolic monarchy, and the Holy Empire—must not mislead us. True, they express the highest aspiration, as well as the great danger of this enterprise, which was to unite in the same community peoples who were so different in their traditions, languages, and level of culture. But the Empire had only just emerged from frightful wars. Christian Europe was extremely small and constantly threatened. A choice had to be made between the politics of conquest and the politics of spiritual understanding. The French Pope chose the latter course. The thought was not new to him, if we may judge by a letter addressed to an unknown correspondent in which he proposes to draw together, and join in a common enterprise devoted to a higher interest, the youthfulness of Robert of France and the youthfulness of Otto III.

Besides, the aged humanist was bound to look with favor upon the rebirth in Rome of a truly imperial court. A government needs a poetic dimension just as much as it needs maxims of statecraft; and those historians who think that people are ruled exclusively by force or by wisdom misjudge the depths of human nature. At the time when Gerbert and Otto made the attempt to revive Roman Europe, it was not foolishness for them to emphasize Roman Europe in formularies and ceremonies. We know the former through the study of seals, the latter from contemporary texts. There are lead seals with the inscriptions IMP. AVG. COS. and SPQR., and even with the figure of a woman, allegory of Rome, and the words: *Renovatio imperii romani*.[6] Through the German chroniclers are very sober, and the Italian chroniclers almost silent, there is a compilation from the second half of the twelfth century, the *Graphia aureae urbis Romae*, quite ill-assorted and even incoherent, which has the merit of containing pieces dating undeniably from the time of Otto III; the original texts have been traced to manuscripts of the eleventh and the end of the tenth centuries. There is, finally, a fragment inserted in another compilation, made by Bonizo of Sutri, concerning the seven palatine judges, which also goes back to the period in which we are interested.[7] The fact that the documents did not always support the allegations of those ancient authors about the judges, and that the latter part of the *Graphia* is full of borrowings from Constantine Porphyrogenitus and swarming with pointless and garbled details concerning the ancient Roman magistratures, detracts in no way from the historical value of the documents insofar as they offer contemporary facts.

The Emperor did not reside in the old palace of the Carolingians which abuts on the Basilica of St. Peter, and which had already been abandoned by his predecessors. He lived in another palace, which we are told was "antique," on the Aventine Hill. The hill where the plebs had seceded, and which, as we have seen, was at

---

[6] For the seals and coins of the year 1000, see especially E. P. Schramm, *Die deutschen Kaiser und Könige in Bildern ihrer Zeit, 751–1152*, Berlin, 1928, pp. 99ff.

[7] F. Picavet, *op. cit.*, pp. 195ff.

the beginning of this century wrapped in a provincial and monastic peace, was at that time the place of residence of the great Roman families. Did the Castello de' Cesari, with its tower, perpetuate the memory of one of these, or even in a confused way the memory of the German Caesars? Not far from it rose the convent of St. Mary of Aventine, which had become the priory of the Order of Malta, and the convent of St. Boniface and St. Alexis, where Latin, Greek, and Slavic monks met together, and where St. Adalbert had retreated before he went to suffer martyrdom in Prussia.[8] This is the monastery to which the Emperor is said to have given the mantle he had worn at his coronation, showing scenes from the Apocalypse embroidered in gold. It is the place from which he set out on his pilgrimages to Monte Gargano or the country of Subiaco, filled with memories of St. Benedict, for his solitary meetings with St. Nil, or his retreats in a cell at St. Clement. From the sublime deprivations of self-denial, he then returned to the splendors of the Empire, and inspired the duties of Empire with an almost religious majesty.[9] His meals were a kind of mass held in solitary splendor. He did not eat, as had his fathers, together with his associates in work and battle, in keeping with the old German custom, but in an isolation that added to the strangeness and magnificence of the stage upon which the table in the shape of a *sigma* was placed. The spirit of Byzantium was surely joined with that of Rome in the ceremonial of a court at which, as we know, one of the dignitaries bore the title of *protospatharios*, another the title of Master of the Militia. Otto, who had been raised by Theophano in a spirit of admiration for learned hierarchies and the splendors of the Greek court, and had been promised in marriage to a Byzantine princess, surely had no need of the advice of some citizen from Ravenna, as has been claimed,

[8] On the relations of St. Adalbert with Otto III, see H. G. Voigt, *Adalbert von Prag. Ein Beitrag zur Geschichte der Kirche und des Mönchstums im zehnten Jahrhundert*, Berlin, 1898.
[9] For the imperial ritual in Rome, see L. Halphen, *La cour d'Otton III à Rome (998–1001)*, *Mélanges d'archéologie et d'histoire de l'École française de Rome*, 1905, pp. 349–363.

to introduce the customs and ceremonial of Constantinople in his own palace. Pontifical Rome itself had felt their influence. Nor do we detract from the authority of the *Graphia* when we point out passages it had borrowed from the *Book of Ceremonies* of Constantine Porphyrogenitus; on the contrary. But the tenor of the scene is above all imperial Roman. Rome is the place where these things take place, and the Roman Empire of the fourth century is what the humanist Pope steeped in Latinity and his disciple wish to restore—restore not as a great achievement of history and archaeology, but through a mixture of traditions and compromises with the changed times. This fact explains not just the titles and the figure on the leaden seals we mentioned earlier, but those processions in white garments, especially striking against the somberly colored background of medieval Italy, which evoke the *togati* of ancient Rome; and the ten gold crowns bearing inscriptions which recall Rome's grandeur and that of her most illustrious emperors.

Does there really exist a new "constitution" like the *Notitia dignitatum* which we find in the *Graphia?* Is it absolutely certain that the ten pontifical judges had become palace judges, each charged with a function of government? Was there a constant and deliberate agreement between the Imperial administration and that of the Apostolic See? The old historians Giesebrecht and Gregorovius believed so, for good reasons. Today there seems to be doubt concerning various matters of detail. But we must not lose sight of the whole picture: and the enterprise certainly remains extraordinary. That enterprise is an almost heroic attempt to create a new framework, a new style of life, and even a modern imperial policy. It is inspired both by an obsession with the past and by the desire to build anew. Can it be said that the Renaissance is arbitrary in its principle, and anti-modern, because it rests on the imitations of the ancient?

We might see a symbol of this Christian resurrection of the ancient Roman Empire in the church which Otto III had built in honor of St. Adalbert, and to which Emile Mâle has devoted several of his finest pages.[10] Today it is the Church of St. Bartholomew, which stands at the southern end of the Tiber island on the site of an ancient temple of Asclepius. It has been reconstructed very frequently, and its façade today is the work of Martino Longhi of the seventeenth century. But it still has fourteen columns of either granite or marble from the temple and the portico which had served Otto's architect. It may well be, as Mâle remarks, that the church no longer exhibits the monumental vastness and nobility of proportion which still distinguished the churches of Paschal I in the ninth century. Fitted into the steps of the choir we find the edge of a narrow well, decorated with figures that belong to a period after the death of Otto III. St. Bartholomew, St. Paulinus of Nola, and Otto III are shown here in the company of Christ.[11] An inscription informs us that this well corresponds to an ancient, holy spring whose water had miraculous healing powers. The Christian faithful have replaced the faithful of Asclepius at the health-bearing fountain. They came among the columns of a dead god to worship the living God. The Emperor himself of the year 1000, too, came to drink from the sacred spring. His dream of Empire, like his little basilica, may have lacked the proper proportions, but the columns of the temple were intact, and standing.

Meanwhile the Italian and the Roman opposition had not put by their weapons. Only a few among the feudal lords were sincerely devoted to the Empire. Yet there were some. The Marquis of Tuscany, Hugh the Great, son of Herbert, had proved his fidelity more than once. Before 996, he had twice visited the im-

[10] E. Mâle, "Études sur les églises romains. L'empereur Otton III à Rome et les églises du Xe siècle," *Revue des Deux Mondes*, September 1937, reprinted in *Rome et ses vieilles églises*, Paris, 1942, pp. 138ff.

[11] On this well, see O. Homburger, *Ein Denkmal ottonischer Plastik in Rom mit dem Bildnis Ottos III, Jahrbuch der preussischen Kunstsammlungen*, 1936, pp. 130ff.; G. de Francovich, "Contributi alla scultura ottoniana in Italia, Il puteale di S. Bartolomeo all' Isola di Roma," *Bolletino d'Arte*, 1936, pp. 207–224. According to these authors, the work dates from the beginning of the eleventh century; according to E. Mâle, *Rome et ses vieilles églises*, pp. 150ff., it is from the twelfth century. There is disagreement also on the identity of the figure of the saint; according to E. Mâle he is St. Paulinus of Nola, according to G. de Francovich, St. Adalbert.

perial court. Was it that Otto's youth seemed to him to favor secret designs or, more plainly, to favor his independence as a great feudal lord, head of a state and almost sovereign? In any event, the House of Saxony looked on him as a sure supporter; and indeed, in times of difficulty we find him near the Emperor, doing his duty. But the princes of the south remained troublesome. Otto III and the papacy were accused of enriching the bishops at the expense of the lords. Did Arduin, marquis of Ivrea, take part in the assassination of the bishop of Verceil (997)? He was accused, and indicted before a council. His properties were seized. This step outraged the North of Italy.

But Rome herself especially remained a menace. Who indeed among the barons and their clients could take an interest in the restoration of the Roman Empire which a king from Germany and a pope born in a foreign country were trying to achieve? Is it to be expected that the assent needed for the success of a great undertaking can be created at one stroke? In this city still smoldering with violent hatreds, the least gust of wind could start a conflagration. And in the early days of 1101, that conflagration bursts into open flame. The inhabitants of Tivoli had risen in revolt against their lord. A pardon was granted them, which greatly irritated Gregory, count of Tusculum. The rebellious nobles collect their bands and come out into the streets. There is fighting. Germans are killed wholesale, the imperial palace on the Aventine is besieged. The emperor, according to Thangmar, is said to have addressed the insurgents from the top of a tower, in this fashion: "Are you the men whom I have called my Romans, the men for the love of whom I have forsaken my homeland, my Saxons, my Germans, my blood? I have adopted you as my sons. And you, in return, cut yourselves off from your father, you have massacred my faithful followers, you drive me out. . . ." And he is said to have spoken further: "I have led you to the remotest corners of our Empire, places that your predecessors had never reached when the entire world was under their command. I have done so to carry your name and your glory to the ends of the earth." [12] Strange words

[12] Thangmar, Vita Bernwardi, cap. 25; see also A. Olleris, op. cit., p. clxxxi.

these, fusing truth with error, words that speak of Germany's border provinces as though they were the latest conquests of the Roman Empire. But doubtless this address was never spoken. It expresses with great plausibility the innermost feelings of Otto III, interpreted with fairness by an intelligent contemporary. But it surely is one of those discourses that the most educated chroniclers had accustomed themselves to inserting into their reports, in the manner of the ancient historians. What follows in Thangmar's narrative makes it clear: moved by the Emperor's words, he goes on, the mob had turned against their own leaders, overpowered them, and cast them at the Emperor's feet. As a matter of fact, Otto III was forced to leave Rome; henceforth we see him wander about Italy, sorely disappointed in his vision. He stays at Ravenna; perhaps Odilo there urged him to return to Germany, as he himself had considered doing for a moment. He moves on to Monte Gargano, then hastens to chastise Benevento. On December 27, 1001, a council opens in Todi, convened to settle the differences between Bernward bishop of Hildesheim and Willigis archbishop of Mainz, concerning their rights on the monastery at Gandersheim. But the bishops who had been called did not arrive. On January 13, they still had not come; that same day Thangmar took leave of the Emperor. It was a critical moment. Up in Germany, there were conspiracies among dukes, counts, and bishops. Otto III was at the end of his strength. The arrival of the archbishop of Cologne and the bishop of Constance is said to have given him some small comfort. He moved on once more, but had to stop, overcome by illness, not far from Rome, the city he could not enter, in the castle of Paterno at the foot of Mount Soracte. There he died, on January 23. Was Gerbert with him during his last moments? His name does not appear in the list of those present. He was to survive him sixteen months.

Such was the end of this admirable and chimerical attempt, of which men may dream for years to come. Was it possible, in the year 1000, to revive the Empire in the midst of a feudal world, to join together the framework of a spiritual structure, built at the

expense of German strength, at the expense of the recently converted barbarian kingdoms? Though their hearts were as one, was
not there a contradiction in the nature of these two men, the
young Parsifal and his master, this Pope in his declining years,
consumed perhaps by his very adroitness? It certainly appears that
they loved and supported each other constantly, that each needed
the other, that they were both passionately devoted to the same
idea. It might well be that the Sovereign Pontiff, in his wisdom,
felt respectful regrets that he had to rule the world together with
an archangel. It might be also that he thought at times how
dangerous was the Greek spark, and how beneficial that Saxon
rusticity. But of this we know absolutely nothing. So much is certain: it was not possible to associate Italy and Germany in this
manner. Because she gave birth to the Empire of the Caesars, Italy
will forever recall to her own mind Vergil's verse: "Roman, remember that it is your birthright to rule the nations." But that is
impossible, at this moment more than ever. What drives Arduin
to recoup Italy's crown immediately on Otto's death, and what
drives the barons to recoup this crown as soon as Sylvester II has
died, is primarily the spirit of outraged feudalism. Henry II will
have to wait ten years for the emperor's crown. Is there a place
from which so large a strife-torn realm may be governed? Aix-la-
Chapelle? But that is too far from the peninsula. Rome? Rome is
too distant from Germany and the marches of the Slavic regions.
A few brilliant successes must not blind us to the paradox inherent
in the situation. In the year 1000, a saint together with a man of
genius could not establish universal rule. The nostalgia of the
Empire, Europe's golden dream of happiness, peace and harmony,
could not overcome the disorder, hatred, and strife that stemmed
from the barbarian invasions. But in the world of the spirit, the
world of culture and of art, tremendous forces arise to overcome
the political factions; and their very diversity, in peaceful times,
becomes the workshop which builds churches and a kind of universal society that is tinged, but not destroyed, by human passion.

Index

71 72 73 74   12 11 10 9 8 7 6 5 4 3 2 1

hARpER ⚜ ꚍORChBOOKS

American Studies: General

HENRY ADAMS Degradation of the Democratic Dogma. ‡ *Introduction by Charles Hirschfeld.* TB/1450

LOUIS D. BRANDEIS: Other People's Money, *and How the Bankers Use It. Ed. with Intro, by Richard M. Abrams* TB/3081

HENRY STEELE COMMAGER, Ed.: The Struggle for Racial Equality TB/1300

CARL N. DEGLER: Out of Our Past: *The Forces that Shaped Modern America* CN/2

CARL N. DEGLER, Ed.: Pivotal Interpretations of American History
Vol. I TB/1240; Vol. II TB/1241

LAWRENCE H. FUCHS, Ed.: American Ethnic Politics TB/1368

ROBERT L. HEILBRONER: The Limits of American Capitalism TB/1305

JOHN HIGHAM, Ed.: The Reconstruction of American History TB/1068

ROBERT H. JACKSON: The Supreme Court in the American System of Government TB/1106

JOHN F. KENNEDY: A Nation of Immigrants. *Illus. Revised and Enlarged. Introduction by Robert F. Kennedy* TB/1118

RICHARD B. MORRIS: Fair Trial: *Fourteen Who Stood Accused, from Anne Hutchinson to Alger Hiss* TB/1335

GUNNAR MYRDAL: An American Dilemma: *The Negro Problem and Modern Democracy. Introduction by the Author.*
Vol. I TB/1443; Vol. II TB/1444

GILBERT OSOFSKY, Ed.: The Burden of Race: *A Documentary History of Negro-White Relations in America* TB/1405

ARNOLD ROSE: The Negro in America: *The Condensed Version of Gunnar Myrdal's* An American Dilemma. Second Edition TB/3048

JOHN E. SMITH: Themes in American Philosophy: *Purpose, Experience and Community* TB/1466

WILLIAM R. TAYLOR: Cavalier and Yankee: *The Old South and American National Character* TB/1474

American Studies: Colonial

BERNARD BAILYN: The New England Merchants in the Seventeenth Century † TB/1149

ROBERT E. BROWN: Middle-Class Democracy and Revolution in Massachusetts, 1691–1780. *New Introduction by Author* TB/1413

JOSEPH CHARLES: The Origins of the American Party System TB/1049

WESLEY FRANK CRAVEN: The Colonies in Transition: 1660-1712† TB/3084

CHARLES GIBSON: Spain in America † TB/3077

CHARLES GIBSON, Ed.: The Spanish Tradition in America + HR/1351

LAWRENCE HENRY GIPSON: The Coming of the Revolution: 1763-1775. † *Illus.* TB/3007

JACK P. GREENE, Ed.: Great Britain and the American Colonies: 1606-1763. + *Introduction by the Author* HR/1477

AUBREY C. LAND, Ed.: Bases of the Plantation Society + HR/1429

PERRY MILLER: Errand Into the Wilderness TB/1139

PERRY MILLER & T. H. JOHNSON, Ed.: The Puritans: *A Sourcebook of Their Writings*
Vol. I TB/1093; Vol. II TB/1094

EDMUND S. MORGAN: The Puritan Family: *Religion and Domestic Relations in Seventeenth Century New England* TB/1227

WALLACE NOTESTEIN: The English People on the Eve of Colonization: 1603-1630. † *Illus.* TB/3006

LOUIS B. WRIGHT: The Cultural Life of the American Colonies: 1607-1763. † *Illus.* TB/3005

YVES F. ZOLTVANY, Ed.: The French Tradition in America + HR/1425

American Studies: The Revolution to 1860

JOHN R. ALDEN: The American Revolution: 1775-1783. † *Illus.* TB/3011

RAY A. BILLINGTON: The Far Western Frontier: 1830-1860. † *Illus.* TB/3012

STUART BRUCHEY: The Roots of American Economic Growth, 1607-1861: *An Essay in Social Causation. New Introduction by the Author.* TB/1350

NOBLE E. CUNNINGHAM, JR., Ed.: The Early Republic, 1789-1828 + HR/1394

GEORGE DANGERFIELD: The Awakening of American Nationalism, 1815-1828. † *Illus.* TB/3061

---

† The New American Nation Series, edited by Henry Steele Commager and Richard B. Morris.
‡ American Perspectives series, edited by Bernard Wishy and William E. Leuchtenburg.
a History of Europe series, edited by J. H. Plumb.
§ The Library of Religion and Culture, edited by Benjamin Nelson.
‖ Researches in the Social, Cultural, and Behavioral Sciences, edited by Benjamin Nelson.
Σ Harper Modern Science Series, edited by James A. Newman.
° Not for sale in Canada.
+ Documentary History of the United States series, edited by Richard B. Morris.
# Documentary History of Western Civilization series, edited by Eugene C. Black and Leonard W. Levy.
Λ The Economic History of the United States series, edited by Henry David et al.
¶ European Perspectives series, edited by Eugene C. Black.
** Contemporary Essays series, edited by Leonard W. Levy.
* The Stratum Series, edited by John Hale.

CLEMENT EATON: The Freedom-of-Thought Struggle in the Old South. *Revised and Enlarged. Illus.* TB/1150

CLEMENT EATON: The Growth of Southern Civilization, 1790-1860. † *Illus.* TB/3040

ROBERT H. FERRELL, Ed.: Foundations of American Diplomacy, 1775-1872 + HR/1393

LOUIS FILLER: The Crusade against Slavery: 1830-1860. † *Illus.* TB/3029

WILLIM W. FREEHLING: Prelude to Civil War: *The Nullification Controversy in South Carolina, 1816-1836* TB/1359

PAUL W. GATES: The Farmer's Age: *Agriculture, 1815-1860* △ TB/1398

THOMAS JEFFERSON: Notes on the State of Virginia. ‡ *Edited by Thomas P. Abernethy* TB/3052

FORREST MCDONALD, Ed.: Confederation and Constitution, 1781-1789 + HR/1396

JOHN C. MILLER: The Federalist Era: 1789-1801. † *Illus.* TB/3027

RICHARD B. MORRIS: The American Revolution Reconsidered TB/1363

CURTIS P. NETTELS: The Emergence of a National Economy, 1775-1815 △ TB/1438

DOUGLASS C. NORTH & ROBERT PAUL THOMAS, Eds.: *The Growth of the American Economy ot 1860* + HR/1352

R. B. NYE: The Cultural Life of the New Nation: 1776-1830. † *Illus.* TB/3026

GILBERT OSOFSKY, Ed.: Puttin' On Ole Massa: *The Slave Narratives of Henry Bibb, William Wells Brown, and Solomon Northup* ‡ TB/1432

JAMES PARTON: The Presidency of Andrew Jackson. *From Volume III of the Life of Andrew Jackson. Ed. with Intro. by Robert V. Remini* TB/3080

FRANCIS S. PHILBRICK: The Rise of the West, 1754-1830. † *Illus.* TB/3067

MARSHALL SMELSER: The Democratic Republic, 1801-1815 † TB/1406

JACK M. SOSIN, Ed.: The Opening of the West + HR/1424

GEORGE ROGERS TAYLOR: The Transportation Revolution, 1815-1860 △ TB/1347

A. F. TYLER: Freedom's Ferment: *Phases of American Social History from the Revolution to the Outbreak of the Civil War. Illus.* TB/1074

GLYNDON G. VAN DEUSEN: The Jacksonian Era: 1828-1848. † *Illus.* TB/3028

LOUIS B. WRIGHT: Culture on the Moving Frontier TB/1053

American Studies: The Civil War to 1900

W. R. BROCK: An American Crisis: *Congress and Reconstruction, 1865-67* ° TB/1283

T. C. COCHRAN & WILLIAM MILLER: The Age of Enterprise: *A Social History of Industrial America* TB/1054

W. A. DUNNING: Reconstruction, Political and Economic: 1865-1877 TB/1073

HAROLD U. FAULKNER: Politics, Reform and Expansion: 1890-1900. † *Illus.* TB/3020

GEORGE M. FREDRICKSON: The Inner Civil War: *Northern Intellectuals and the Crisis of the Union* TB/1358

JOHN A. GARRATY: The New Commonwealth, 1877-1890 † TB/1410

JOHN A. GARRATY, Ed.: The Transformation of American Society, 1870-1890 + HR/1395

HELEN HUNT JACKSON: A Century of Dishonor: *The Early Crusade for Indian Reform.* † *Edited by Andrew F. Rolle* TB/3063

WILLIAM G. MCLOUGHLIN, Ed.: The American Evangelicals, 1800-1900: An Anthology ‡ TB/1382

JAMES S. PIKE: The Prostrate State: *South Carolina under Negro Government.* ‡ *Intro. by Robert F. Durden* TB/3085

FRED A. SHANNON: The Farmer's Last Frontier: *Agriculture, 1860-1897* TB/1348

VERNON LANE WHARTON: The Negro in Mississippi, 1865-1890 TB/1178

American Studies: The Twentieth Century

RICHARD M. ABRAMS, Ed.: The Issues of the Populist and Progressive Eras, 1892-1912 + HR/1428

RAY STANNARD BAKER: Following the Color Line: *American Negro Citizenship in Progressive Era.* ‡ *Edited by Dewey W. Grantham, Jr. Illus.* TB/3053

RANDOLPH S. BOURNE: War and the Intellectuals: *Collected Essays, 1915-1919.* ‡ *Edited by Carl Resek* TB/3043

A. RUSSELL BUCHANAN: The United States and World War II. † *Illus.* Vol. I TB/3044; Vol. II TB/3045

THOMAS C. COCHRAN: The American Business System: *A Historical Perspective, 1900-1955* TB/1080

FOSTER RHEA DULLES: America's Rise to World Power: 1898-1954. † *Illus.* TB/3021

HAROLD U. FAULKNER: The Decline of Laissez Faire, 1897-1917 TB/1397

JOHN D. HICKS: Republican Ascendancy: 1921-1933. † *Illus.* TB/3041

WILLIAM E. LEUCHTENBURG: Franklin D. Roosevelt and the New Deal: 1932-1940. † *Illus.* TB/3025

WILLIAM E. LEUCHTENBURG, Ed.: The New Deal: *A Documentary History* + HR/1354

ARTHUR S. LINK: Woodrow Wilson and the Progressive Era: 1910-1917. † *Illus.* TB/3023

BROADUS MITCHELL: Depression Decade: *From New Era through New Deal, 1929-1941* △ TB/1439

GEORGE E. MOWRY: The Era of Theodore Roosevelt and the Birth of Modern America: 1900-1912. † *Illus.* TB/3022

GEORGE SOULE: Prosperity Decade: *From War to Depression, 1917-1929* △ TB/1349

TWELVE SOUTHERNERS: I'll Take My Stand: *The South and the Agrarian Tradition. Intro. by Louis D. Rubin, Jr.; Biographical Essays by Virginia Rock* TB/1072

Art, Art History, Aesthetics

ERWIN PANOFSKY: Renaissance and Renascences in Western Art. *Illus.* TB/1447

ERWIN PANOFSKY: Studies in Iconology: *Humanistic Themes in the Art of the Renaissance. 180 illus.* TB/1077

OTTO VON SIMSON: The Gothic Cathedral: *Origins of Gothic Architecture and the Medieval Concept of Order. 58 illus.* TB/2018

HEINRICH ZIMMER: Myths and Symbols in Indian Art and Civilization. *70 illus.* TB/2005

Asian Studies

WOLFGANG FRANKE: China and the West: *The Cultural Encounter, 13th to 20th Centuries. Trans. by R. A. Wilson* TB/1326

L. CARRINGTON GOODRICH: A Short History of the Chinese People. *Illus.* TB/3015

2

3

4

KARL R. POPPER: The Open Society and Its Enemies *Vol. I: The Spell of Plato* TB/1101 *Vol. II: The High Tide of Prophecy: Hegel, Marx, and the Aftermath* TB/1102
HENRI DE SAINT-SIMON: Social Organization, The Science of Man, and Other Writings. || *Edited and Translated with an Introduction by Felix Markham* TB/1152
JOSEPH A. SCHUMPETER: Capitalism, Socialism and Democracy TB/3008

Psychology

LUDWIG BINSWANGER: Being-in-the-World: *Selected Papers.* || *Trans. with Intro. by Jacob Needleman* TB/1365
HADLEY CANTRIL: The Invasion from Mars: *A Study in the Psychology of Panic* || TB/1282
MIRCEA ELIADE: Cosmos and History: *The Myth of the Eternal Return §* TB/2050
MIRCEA ELIADE: Myth and Reality TB/1369
MIRCEA ELIADE: Myths, Dreams and Mysteries: *The Encounter Between Contemporary Faiths and Archaic Realities §* TB/1320
MIRCEA ELIADE: Rites and Symbols of Initiation: *The Mysteries of Birth and Rebirth §* TB/1236
SIGMUND FREUD: On Creativity and the Unconscious: *Papers on the Psychology of Art, Literature, Love, Religion. § Intro. by Benjamin Nelson* TB/45
J. GLENN GRAY: The Warriors: *Reflections on Men in Battle. Introduction by Hannah Arendt* TB/1294
WILLIAM JAMES: Psychology: *The Briefer Course. Edited with an Intro. by Gordon Allport* TB/1034
KARL MENNINGER, M.D.: Theory of Psychoanalytic Technique TB/1144

Religion: Ancient and Classical, Biblical and Judaic Traditions

MARTIN BUBER: Eclipse of God: *Studies in the Relation Between Religion and Philosophy* TB/12
MARTIN BUBER: Hasidism and Modern Man. *Edited and Translated by Maurice Friedman* TB/839
MARTIN BUBER: The Knowledge of Man. *Edited with an Introduction by Maurice Friedman. Translated by Maurice Friedman and Ronald Gregor Smith* TB/135
MARTIN BUBER: Moses. *The Revelation and the Covenant* TB/837
MARTIN BUBER: The Origin and Meaning of Hasidism. *Edited and Translated by Maurice Friedman* TB/835
MARTIN BUBER: The Prophetic Faith TB/73
MARTIN BUBER: Two Types of Faith: *Interpenetration of Judaism and Christianity °* TB/75
MALCOLM L. DIAMOND: Martin Buber: *Jewish Existentialist* TB/840
M. S. ENSLIN: Christian Beginnings TB/5
M. S. ENSLIN: The Literature of the Christian Movement TB/6
HENRI FRANKFORT: Ancient Egyptian Religion: *An Interpretation* TB/77
ABRAHAM HESCHEL: God in Search of Man: *A Philosophy of Judaism* TB/807
ABRAHAM HESCHEL: Man Is not Alone: *A Philosophy of Religion* TB/838
T. J. MEEK: Hebrew Origins TB/69
H. J. ROSE: Religion in Greece and Rome TB/55

Religion: Early Christianity Through Reformation

ANSELM OF CANTERBURY: Truth, Freedom, and Evil: *Three Philosophical Dialogues. Edited and Translated by Jasper Hopkins and Herbert Richardson* TB/317
JOHANNES ECKHART: Meister Eckhart: *A Modern Translation by R. Blakney* TB/8
EDGAR J. GOODSPEED: A Life of Jesus TB/1
ROBERT M. GRANT: Gnosticism and Early Christianity TB/136
ARTHUR DARBY NOCK: St. Paul ° TR/104
GORDON RUPP: Luther's Progress to the Diet of Worms ° TB/120

Religion: The Protestant Tradition

KARL BARTH: Church Dogmatics: *A Selection. Intro. by H. Gollwitzer. Ed. by G. W. Bromiley* TB/95
KARL BARTH: Dogmatics in Outline TB/56
KARL BARTH: The Word of God and the Word of Man TB/13
WILLIAM R. HUTCHISON, Ed.: American Protestant Thought: *The Liberal Era* ‡ TB/1385
SOREN KIERKEGAARD: Edifying Discourses. *Edited with an Intro. by Paul Holmer* TB/32
SOREN KIERKEGAARD: The Journals of Kierkegaard. ° *Edited with an Intro. by Alexander Dru* TB/52
SOREN KIERKEGAARD: The Point of View for My Work as an Author: *A Report to History. § Preface by Benjamin Nelson* TB/88
SOREN KIERKEGAARD: The Present Age. § *Translated and edited by Alexander Dru. Introduction by Walter Kaufmann* TB/94
SOREN KIERKEGAARD: Purity of Heart. *Trans. by Douglas Steere* TB/4
SOREN KIERKEGAARD: Repetition: *An Essay in Experimental Psychology §* TB/117
WOLFHART PANNENBERG, et al.: History and Hermeneutic. *Volume 4 of Journal for Theology and the Church, edited by Robert W. Funk and Gerhard Ebeling* TB/254
F. SCHLEIERMACHER: The Christian Faith. *Introduction by Richard R. Niebuhr.*
Vol. I TB/108; Vol. II TB/109
F. SCHLEIERMACHER: On Religion: *Speeches to Its Cultured Despisers. Intro. by Rudolf Otto* TB/36
PAUL TILLICH: Dynamics of Faith TB/42
PAUL TILLICH: Morality and Beyond TB/142

Religion: The Roman & Eastern Christian Traditions

A. ROBERT CAPONIGRI, Ed.: Modern Catholic Thinkers II: *The Church and the Political Order* TB/307
G. P. FEDOTOV: The Russian Religious Mind: *Kievan Christianity, the tenth to the thirteenth Centuries* TB/370
GABRIEL MARCEL: Being and Having: *An Existential Diary. Introduction by James Collins* TB/310
GABRIEL MARCEL: Homo Viator: *Introduction to a Metaphysic of Hope* TB/397

Religion: Oriental Religions

TOR ANDRAE: Mohammed: *The Man and His Faith §* TB/62
EDWARD CONZE: Buddhism: *Its Essence and Development. ° Foreword by Arthur Waley* TB/58

5

EDWARD CONZE et al, Editors: Buddhist Texts through the Ages TB/113
H. G. CREEL: Confucius and the Chinese Way TB/63
FRANKLIN EDGERTON, Trans. & Ed.: The Bhagavad Gita TB/115
SWAMI NIKHILANANDA, Trans. & Ed.: The Upanishads TB/114

Religion: Philosophy, Culture, and Society

NICOLAS BERDYAEV: The Destiny of Man TB/61
RUDOLF BULTMANN: History and Eschatology: *The Presence of Eternity* ° TB/91
LUDWIG FEUERBACH: The Essence of Christianity. § *Introduction by Karl Barth. Foreword by H. Richard Niebuhr* TB/11
ADOLF HARNACK: What Is Christianity? § *Introduction by Rudolf Bultmann* TB/17
KYLE HASELDEN: The Racial Problem in Christian Perspective TB/116
IMMANUEL KANT: Religion Within the Limits of Reason Alone. § *Introduction by Theodore M. Greene and John Silber* TB/67
H. RICHARD NIERUHR: Christ and Culture TB/3
H. RICHARD NIEBUHR: The Kingdom of God in America TB/49

Science and Mathematics

W. E. LE GROS CLARK: The Antecedents of Man: *An Introduction to the Evolution of the Primates.* ° *Illus.* TB/559
ROBERT E. COKER: Streams, Lakes, Ponds. *Illus.* TB/586
ROBERT E. COKER: This Great and Wide Sea: *An Introduction to Oceanography and Marine Biology. Illus.* TB/551
F. K. HARE: The Restless Atmosphere TB/560
WILLARD VAN ORMAN QUINE: Mathematical Logic TB/558

Science: Philosophy

J. M. BOCHENSKI: The Methods of Contemporary Thought. *Tr. by Peter Caws* TB/1377
J. BRONOWSKI: Science and Human Values. *Revised and Enlarged. Illus.* TB/505
WERNER HEISENBERG: Physics and Philosophy: *The Revolution in Modern Science. Introduction by F. S. C. Northrop* TB/549
KARL R. POPPER: Conjectures and Refutations: *The Growth of Scientific Knowledge* TB/1376
KARL R. POPPER: The Logic of Scientific Discovery TB/576

Sociology and Anthropology

REINHARD BENDIX: Work and Authority in Industry: *Ideologies of Management in the Course of Industrialization* TB/3035
BERNARD BERELSON, Ed., The Behavioral Sciences Today TB/1127
KENNETH B. CLARK: Dark Ghetto: *Dilemmas of Social Power. Foreword by Gunnar Myrdal* TB/1317

KENNETH CLARK & JEANNETTE HOPKINS: A Relevant War Against Poverty: *A Study of Community Action Programs and Observable Social Change* TB/1480
LEWIS COSER, Ed.: Political Sociology TB/1293
ALLISON DAVIS & JOHN DOLLARD: Children of Bondage: *The Personality Development of Negro Youih in the Urban South* || TB/3049
ST. CLAIR DRAKE & HORACE R. CAYTON: Black Metropolis: *A Study of Negro Life in a Northern City. Introduction by Everett C. Hughes. Tables, maps, charts, and graphs* Vol. I TB/1086; Vol. II TB/1087
PETER F. DRUCKER: The New Society: The Anatomy of Industrial Order TB/1082
CHARLES Y. GLOCK & RODNEY STARK: Christian Beliefs and Anti-Semitism. *Introduction by the Authors* TB/1454
ALVIN W. GOULDNER: The Hellenic World TB/1479
R. M. MACIVER: Social Causation TB/1153
GARY T. MARX: Protest and Prejudice: *A Study of Belief in the Black Community* TB/1435
ROBERT K. MERTON, LEONARD BROOM, LEONARD S. COTTRELL, JR., Editors: Sociology Today: *Problems and Prospects* || Vol. I TB/1173; Vol. II TB/1174
GILBERT OSOFSKY, Ed.: The Burden of Race: A Documentary History of Negro-White Relations in America TB/1405
GILBERT OSOFSKY: Harlem: The Making of a Ghetto: *Negro New York 1890-1930* TB/1381
TALCOTT PARSONS & EDWARD A. SHILS, Editors: Toward a General Theory of Action: *Theoretical Foundations for the Social Sciences* TB/1083
PHILIP RIEFF: The Triumph of the Therapeutic: *Uses of Faith After Freud* TB/1360
JOHN H. ROHRER & MUNRO S. EDMONSON, Eds.: The Eighth Generation Grows Up: *Cultures and Personalities of New Orleans Negroes* || TB/3050
ARNOLD ROSE: The Negro in America: *The Condensed Version of Gunnar Myrdal's* An American Dilemma. *Second Edition* TB/3048
GEORGE ROSEN: Madness in Society: *Chapters in the Historical Sociology of Mental Illness.* || *Preface by Benjamin Nelson* TB/1337
PHILIP SELZNICK: TVA and the Grass Roots: *A Study in the Sociology of Formal Organization* TB/1230
PITIRIM A. SOROKIN: Contemporary Sociological Theories: *Through the First Quarter of the Twentieth Century* TB/3046
MAURICE R. STEIN: The Eclipse of Community: *An Interpretation of American Studies* TB/1128
FERDINAND TONNIES: Community and Society: *Gemeinschaft und Gesellschaft. Translated and Edited by Charles P. Loomis* TB/1116
W. LLOYD WARNER and Associates: Democracy in Jonesville: *A Study in Quality and Inequality* || TB/1129
W. LLOYD WARNER: Social Class in America: *The Evaluation of Status* TB/1013
FLORIAN ZNANIECKI: The Social Role of the Man of Knowledge. *Introduction by Lewis A. Coser* TB/1372